ACTUALIZING MANAGERIAL ROLES THROUGH CORPORATE LEADERSHIP: EXPLORING INDIAN CORPORATES

ACTUALIZING MANAGERIAL ROLES THROUGH CORPORATE LEADERSHIP: EXPLORING INDIAN CORPORATES

By

Dr. TULIKA SAXENA
Assistant Prof. Head of Department
Department of Management
Rama Group of Institution
Kanpur, Uttar Pradesh

UNIVERSITY SCIENCE PRESS
(An Imprint of Laxmi Publications Pvt. Ltd.)
An ISO 9001:2015 Company
BENGALURU • CHENNAI • GUWAHATI • HYDERABAD • JALANDHAR
KOCHI • KOLKATA • LUCKNOW • MUMBAI • RANCHI
NEW DELHI

ACTUALIZING MANAGERIAL ROLES THROUGH CORPORATE LEADERSHIP: EXPLORING INDIAN CORPORATES

Printed and bound in India
Typeset at : Kalyani Computer Services, New Delhi
First Edition : 2011, *Edition* : 2019
UAM-9388-075-ACTU MANAG ROLE THRO CORP
ISBN : 978-81-318-0733-0

PUBLISHED IN INDIA BY

UNIVERSITY SCIENCE PRESS
(An Imprint of Laxmi Publications Pvt. Ltd.)
An ISO 9001:2015 Company
113, GOLDEN HOUSE, DARYAGANJ,
NEW DELHI - 110002, INDIA
Telephone : 91-11-4353 2500, 4353 2501
Fax : 91-11-2325 2572, 4353 2528
www.laxmipublications.com info@laxmipublications.com

Branches

Bengaluru	080-26 75 69 30	
Chennai	044-24 34 47 26,	24 35 95 07
Guwahati	0361-254 36 69,	251 38 81
Hyderabad	040-27 55 53 83,	27 55 53 93
Jalandhar	0181-222 12 72	
Kochi	0484-237 70 04,	405 13 03
Kolkata	033-22 27 43 84	
Lucknow	0522-220 99 16	
Mumbai	022-24 93 12 61	
Ranchi	0651-220 44 64	

C—00000/019/06
Printed at: L.B. Enterprises, Delhi

Contents

PREFACE

The present scenario is characterized by global competition, fierce quest for excellence, and constant striving to break one's own performance records and establish new performance milestones. The liberalization of Indian economy, privatization and globalization are forcing management to search for better alternatives for survival and success of the organizations. This will necessitate organizational change not once or twice but as many times as the business context shifts. It is in this context that the need for a new brand of corporate leadership is being increasingly felt. What we now need is transformational leadership, capable of effectively projecting and responding to the dynamic environmental demands and challenges. It is this breed of leadership that will build responsive organizations, evolve new ethos and values within organizations and create a culture conducive to corporate transformation.

Since the organization is basically a deliberate creation of human beings for certain specified objectives, the activities of its members need to be directed in a certain way. The importance of good leadership is that it motivates employees, create confidence, give satisfaction, build morale and encourage high performance, high efficiency and effectiveness, productivity and organizational stability. The above are made possible through continued endeavour for self-renewal and relentless preparation by benchmarking with the best performers to enable surpassing established records.

Senior managers are highly sensitive to the cultural nuances, unique to India and sought to incorporate culture-specific modes in bringing about transformation and change. A priority between transactional and transformational functions of leadership is emerging as a crucial challenge for managerial leadership for ensuring the sustained success to an organization in the highly competitive business environment. Leaders must be supported by organizational culture and corporate management to have autonomy to serve in their own style as per need of the situation.

The challenge for the present organizations is to move from transactional leadership to more transformational leadership with the ability to deconstruct the present organization and reconstruct it for the future. Corporations will need leaders who can bring about a transformation; provide leadership through personal power; create a work culture of openness to new ideas, provide freedom for experimentation and exploration; collectivize and carry people along by inspiring them; build multiple leaders, empower, delegate, facilitate, support and play the role of a coach and a mentor; create sense of identity, higher purpose and goal, and provide opportunity for continuous learning, growth and development.

The business scenario in India has undergone an unprecedented sea change at the socio-economics, cultural, political and technological levels. Use of managerial authority in the form of transactional leadership is not bringing the desired results. The primary role of the senior management as policy-formulator, strategic thinker, and visionary planner has been reduced to that of mere implementers of policy directed by bureaucrats, politicians and management. No wonder then, many chief executives in the public as well as private sector enterprises do not believe in taking adequate initiative, accountability and risk.

The organization cannot sit comfortably with the policies and practices and has to give a fresh look for increasing effectiveness in the role performance of leaders serving as managers. In sum, it can be reiterated that it should be left to the individual manager, how to conceptualize and plan his/her role to evolve a leadership (transformational) framework within the managerial (transactional) functions.

Chapterization: A Profile

The present work is organized into five chapters. Chapter I presents a synoptical view of the study on corporate leadership as related to role efficacy in select Indian organizations. Chapter II portrays the conceptual framework of corporate leadership and role efficacy. Chapter III presents methodology. Chapter IV examines data analysis and results. Finally, Chapter V presents conclusion and suggestions.

—AUTHOR

ACKNOWLEDGEMENT

The credit for the work goes to my guide Dr. B.L. Bajpai, who gave me the opportunity to undertake this research and always extended his best possible help and guidance in the completion of this work.

Words cannot express the sense of gratitude and indebtedness, I owe to Dr. Aniurudh Pandey who always inspired and encouraged me to put all the efforts to make the work valuable for different organizations. His insightful guidance enabled me to complete this work.

I wish to record my deep sense of gratitude to professor, Dr. Udai Pareek, who permitted me to use his Role Efficacy Scale and Senior Managers Functions Schedule for this research.

I wish to record my sense of gratitude to Sri S.K Mandal, scientist-E, statistics & biometry section of C.D.R.I., Lucknow, who helped me in selecting and adapting suitable techniques for treatment of the data.

I take this opportunity to express my sincere thanks to Dr. J K Sharma, Head of the Department MBA, Lucknow University, for his co-operation throughout the investigation.

I am immensely indebted to professor Dr S.G Bhargava, Professor, IIT Mumbai, for providing me guidance, constructive suggestions and necessary inputs through fruitful discussions at all stages.

I am highly obliged to (*i*) National Fertilizers Limited (NFL), Vijaipur (M.P.), (*ii*) Sahara India Pariwar, Lucknow, (*iii*) Provincial Medical & Health Services (PMHS), Doctors, Gonda (U.P), (*iv*) Lohia Machines Limited (LML), Kanpur and (*v*) Uttar Pradesh Power Corporation Limited (UPPCL), Kanpur, for giving me the opportunity to conduct the study in their esteemed organizations. I am thankful to all the company executives and employees for their kind help and co-operation.

I wish to avail this opportunity of thanking the staff members of Department of Business Administration, Lucknow University for their help and co-operation.

Finally, I owe special gratitude to my beloved family who charged me with the spirit and enthusiasm to produce this work with more vigor and perfection.

List of Tables

Chapter 1

SYNOPTICAL VIEW OF THE STUDY

INTRODUCTION

Leadership is about understanding people, and especially about the process of making a real connect with potential workforce. Corporate leadership is perceived in divergent ways. Some explain success in terms of profit, productivity, and capacity utilization; others relate it to the market share, sales-growth, turnover and yet others to human satisfaction. The role of managerial leadership is to build the shared vision, empower the people, serve as exemplars, create trust and confidence, generate commitment, promote teamwork, facilitate collaborative problem-solving, care and concern, encourage receptivity and openness, promoting total development and growth of people, and strengthen a culture of continuous learning, besides steering the enterprise in pursuit of its values and vision.

Perhaps, endeavor of this study is to examine corporate leadership through role efficacy practiced by senior management. Difference in philosophies of various organizations put a limit on the person being a good manager or a good leader, or both. To successfully create a peak performance, organizations need strong management, that is, knowledgeable, experienced, skillful managers who know the business inside and out and who are able and willing to make the right strategic decision and management makes sure those decisions are implemented. Organizations also need strong leadership, people who can influence the behaviours, norms, values, attitudes, and the willingness of the whole organization to peak perform. The best situation occurs when the same person fills the role of both these function. Organizations expectations regarding the leader's styles are manifestations of certain culturally valued behaviour; it is desirable to study it in order to evolve a kind of organizational culture, where corporate management must give autonomy to managers to serve in their own style as per need of the situation, which could be culturally consistent and functional in the Indian context.

Exploring a leader's role and operating leadership style in an organization gives an understanding of organizational dynamics, its culture, its structure, its various systems, interlinkages, hierarchical levels and associated processes. As far as role efficacy is concerned, it is the most basic and elementary concept in understanding success of an organization as it determines individual efficiency in the organizational context. It is through role that an individual gets linked with the organizational system. The involvement and integration of individual with the role creates joy in the work he does, and builds a strong sense of commitment and citizenship to the organization.

Leaders instill a philosophy, provide new meaning to managerial actions and raise the collective consciousness of organizational members. These help significantly in mobilizing organizational resources and channellising them for organizational transformation. Chief executive/ senior manager has to perform dual role. On one hand, he is chief liaison officer between board and other personnel of the organization and provides information about what board has decided in terms of organizational goals, policies, etc., on the other hand, he is the chief executive officer to execute these policies and programmes into action. Ironically enough, however the present industrial society seems to suffer from an unprecedented crisis of transformational leadership at the senior level, though they are performing satisfactorily on transactional leadership functions. Since, managerial styles are determined by a host of factors such as forces in corporate policy makers, existing culture and climate, degree of autonomy and discretion given to the senior managers, it is unlikely to expect a uniform leadership styles in every organizations.

Indian organizations are generally top management centered, where not only middle and lower managerial cadre, but senior managerial cadre is also being closely supervised by the top management and only a limited degree of participation is allowed. However the real situation in this context can be appreciated only when a detailed account of various practices is taken for consideration. Fortunately, some empirical studies are available in this context, which do not necessarily support this view rather they present a mixed note.

In family managed traditional organizations the most prevalent style is autocratic. These organizations are highly centralized in their organizational structure and are authoritarian in their approach. On the other hand, there are many organizations in the private sector owned by Indians that have appreciable degree of participation and democratic style. The third category of organization is public sector. Here, bureaucratic style is more prevalent owing to the work culture inherited by public managers. Its implication is status differentials, class distinctions, and impersonal relationships, which work against participative style.

The capacity of the organization to make a paradigmatic shift depends upon its capacity to continuously "transform". The organization cannot sit comfortably with the policies and practices and has to give a fresh look for increasing effectiveness in the role performance of leaders. In sum, it can be reiterated that it should be left to the individual senior manager, how to conceptualize and plan his/her role to evolve a leadership (transformational) framework within the managerial (transactional) functions.

The central theme of this work has been the study of style and value profile of leaders, which builds the organization. The two forms of leadership styles are not entirely mutually exclusive; leaders are not necessarily one or the other, but both. The transformational leaders perceive their capability basically in terms of managing human beings through empowering attitude, team building and evoking a sense of confidence, visioning, modeling/Inspiring, setting standards and boundary management etc. These transformational functions should be appropriately coupled with transactional functions through entrepreneurial risk-taking, not losing balance, clarity of organizational goals and capability to plan for the future, policy making, developing systems, monitoring performances, coordinating, rewarding and coaching, synergising, developing talent/ mentoring and building culture and climate.

DEFINING LEADERSHIP

Leadership is the process of influencing the behaviour of others to work willingly and enthusiastically for achieving predetermined goals. The successful organization has one major attribute that sets it apart from unsuccessful organization is dynamic and effective leadership.

"Leadership has been conceived as the focus of group processes, as a matter of personality, as a matter of inducing compliance, as the exercise of influence, as particular behaviours, as a form of persuasion, as a power relation, as an instrument to achieve goals, as an effect of interaction, as a differentiated role, as initiation of structure, and as many combinations of these definitions" **(Bass & Stogdil, 1990).**

"Leadership is interpersonal influence exercised in a situation and directed through communication process, towards the attainment of a specified goal or goals" (**Tannenbaum**, 1961).

"Leadership is essentially a continuous process of influencing behaviors. A leader breathes life into the group and motivates it towards goals. The lukewarm desires for achievement are transformed into a burning passion for accomplishment" (**Terry**, 1988).

"Leaders should lead not only through knowledge, competence and skill but through vision, courage, responsibility and integrity" (**Drucker**, 1955).

"The leader is responsible for the set of ethics or norms that govern the behaviour of people in the organization" (**Bennis** and **Nanus**, 1985).

"Leader should be reliable. Reliability is a primary sign of the grown-up executive" (**Crosby**, 1990).

"The Leader is believed to have the capacity to influence the people within his organization to high performance" (**Kotter**, 1990).

Robbins (1983) defined *"Leadership as the ability of the leader to influence a group toward the achievement of its goals"*.

"The ability of the leader to influence individuals into some deliberate and meaningful action" (**Ivancevich & Matteson**, 1996).

"Awareness is the seed for transformation. Nothing changes without personal transformation," believes **W. Edwards Deming** (1986).

"Leadership has been defined in terms of traits, behavior, contingency, power, and occupation of an administrative position. Leadership is by nature is dialectical. The literature also debates upon the differences between managers and leaders such as managers do thing right and leaders right things" (**Bennis**, 1989).

"Managers develop plan while leaders create a vision and strategy to achieve them. Managers organize and engage themselves in the process of controlling and problem solving and leaders engage in a process of alignment and seek to motivate and inspire" (**Kotter**, 1996).

Peters and **Waterman** (1982) have argued *"an effective leader must be the master of two ends of the spectrum—ideas at the highest level of obstruction and action at the most mundane level of detail"*.

One of the most significant transitions in management thinking in recent years has been a shift in emphasis in the context of managerial leadership from management to leadership. In an article published in Harvard Business Review entitled, *Managers and Leaders: Are They Different?* **Abraham Zaleznik** highlights a watershed in the conceptual understanding of "leadership as a function distinct from that of management (Zaleznik, 1986). One important dimension of Zaleznik's research finding is that managers tend to adopt impersonal attitudes toward goals whereas leaders bring into play a personal and active attitude while seeking their goals".

In the introduction to a recent issue of the Journal of Applied Behavioural Sciences, the Editor (R. E. Kaplan) tells us that" leadership entails not just a change of behaviour but also a more fundamental change in character and identity".

"Yet, despite all the attention given to it and its recognized importance, leadership still remains pretty much of a "black box," or unexplainable concept. It is known to exist and to have a tremendous influence on human performance, but its inner workings and specific dimensions cannot be precisely spelled out. Leadership has probably been written about, formally researched, and informally discussed more than any other single topic (**Luthans**, 1984)."

The strategies for transformational leadership could be: Attention through vision, meaning through communication, trust through positioning, deployment of self (**Bennis & Nanus**, 1985). Tichy & Devanna (1986) recognizing the need for revitalization, creating a new vision, institutionalizing change. Kouzes & Posner (1987) challenging the process, inspiring a shared vision, enabling other to act, modeling the way and encouraging the heart. Nadler & Tushman (1989) Envisioning, energizing, enabling, structuring, controlling and rewarding. **Conger**, (1989) Detecting unexploited opportunities and deficiencies in the current situation communicating the vision, building trust, demonstrating the means to achieve the vision. **Nevis** (1996) Persuasive communication, participation, expectancy, role modeling, structural rearrangement and extrinsic rewards coercion.

TYPOLOGIES AND TAXONOMIES OF LEADERSHIP

Different types of leaders have been studied according to the groups they lead. The types of leaders studied have included college presidents, chief executive officers, military officers, school principals, student leaders, task leaders, technical leaders, hospital and nursing administrators, religious leaders, revolutionaries, leaders of crowds, criminal leaders, managers at all levels in business and industry, consumer-opinion leaders, experimental small-group leaders, women leaders, black leaders, public officials, athletic leaders, child and adolescent leaders, civic leaders, musical leaders, charitable leaders, leaders of social movements, political leaders (heads of state or government), and administrators at all levels of various public agencies and private institutions. Typologies have been created within and among these specializations.

Defining Role-Efficacy

The concept of Role -Efficacy was originally initiated by **Kahn & Associates** (1964). According to Udai Pareek (1987), when an individual joins an organization, he is appraised of the duties which he has to perform. At the same time, he projects his own expectations from the role. The performance of a person working in an organization depends on his own potential effectiveness as a person, his technical competence, his managerial experience, etc., as well as the way the role which he performs in the organization is designed. It is the integration of the two (the person and the role) that ensures the person's effectiveness in the organization. Role-efficacy would mean the potential effectiveness of an individual occupying a particular role in an organization, as he perceives it in the constellation of various other significant roles.

Statement of the Problem

Leadership is the premier force governing success of any organization. In recent scenario increasing attention has been paid to how and when we perceive leadership to be important.

Leaders are symbolic figures whose deeds are out of the ordinary. They show that ideal of success lies with-in human capacity, that peoples simply work a little harder because they are dedicated to the cause, let it be corporate leadership. If values are the soul of the culture, then transformational leadership personify those values and epitomize the strength of the organization as leader is a person whom everyone counts on when things get tough.

Not only do role-efficacy recognizes the corporate leadership but also organizational culture fosters the development of the same.

EXPECTED CONTRIBUTIONS FROM THE STUDY

There are following expected contributions from the synoptical view of study:

1. The study will benchmark to certain paths of progress for corporate sector for attaining corporate leadership.
2. The study will bring cultural metamorphosis in the organizations by making senior managers to practice not only the transactional leadership but also the transformational leadership style in their organizations.
3. The study will provide information to the organization to transform into the center of excellence and enhance productivity and effectiveness with voluntary contribution of organizational members.
4. The study may serve as a guide to identify sources available in organizational setup for enhancing transformational leadership in the corporate world.
5. The study may open a new horizon that transformational leaders survive as leading legends in the global stand and make it easy to for organizations to confront unprecedented challenges.
6. The research will enhance contributions of senior managers in the organizations and will overall enhance job satisfaction, motivation and commitment of the workforce.

Chapter 2

ACTUALIZING MANAGERIAL ROLES THROUGH CORPORATE LEADERSHIP—CONCEPTUAL FRAMEWORK

INTRODUCING CORPORATE LEADERSHIP

In the present state of rapid changes taking place every moment the leader is construed as strategist, is portrayed as hero, to unite and motivate his followers by offering shared goals for a better tomorrow. Leadership is to be structured in terms of totality of functions performed by executives as individuals and as a group.

A review of foregoing discussions, leads us to accept that a corporate manager has to function, both as a leader and as a manager *i.e.,* he has to perform transformational as well as transactional functions. Transactional functions are primarily concerned with achievement of tasks and work is done on the basis of agreed plans, and a contract to reward people for good work is the key component. Leaders have an obligation to get things done, ensure achievement of targets and maximize efficiency and effectiveness of the organization as a whole. Transformational functions on the other hand are primarily concerned with getting, performance from people beyond expectations, by going beyond the contractual relationship by inspiring them, stimulating them and paying attention to them.

Leadership Functions

Leaders need to perform both transactional and transformational functions, for which a list of the main functions were prepared and classified into two groups: transactional and transformational.

Transactional Functions

Leaders have an obligation to get things done, ensure achievement of targets and maximize efficiency and effectiveness of various groups. Transactional function includes following dimensions:

(i) Policy Making: This is an important leadership function. The leader arranges to set priorities and directions for organizational work, and create linkages among several aspects of the organization. These are reflected in the policies developed as a guiding force in the organization. The policy comes out of the organization's vision and mission.

(ii) Planning: The next logical step is to plan various activities in order to translate policies into action. Planning involves working out detailed action steps, the needed resources, and contingency arrangements if a proposed action does not get done.

(iii) Developing Systems: Organizational leaders work towards institutionalization of practices and change. This can be done by developing systems on various aspects of the organization. Systems economize energy and lead to faster action like through management information system, budgetary system, human resource development system, reward system etc.

(iv) Monitoring Performance: Managerial control of workforce requires effective monitoring, one of the most important functions of senior managers. Monitoring is done against the accepted standards and agreed plans.

(v) Coordinating: When individuals and groups work in synergy, duplication is avoided and mutual support is ensured.

(vi) Rewarding: Senior managers reward good performance of exemplary behaviour of individuals and teams. This reinforces their behaviour, and also the behaviour of others.

(vii) Coaching: One of the functions of senior manager is to guide their juniors through performance counselling and coaching. This includes helping them to know their own strengths and weaknesses and improve their performance in future.

Transformational Functions

While transactional functions are primarily concerned with achievement of tasks, transformational functions go beyond the immediate task and build individuals and groups and enable them to achieve targets that the organization or individual would never have expected. These functions increase power in the organization by empowering various groups and individuals. The following functions fall in this category:

(i) Visioning: The management cadre creates vision for the organization. Vision is the dream, which inspires people and makes them proud of working in the organization.

(ii) Modeling: A way to inspire people is to set a personal example of a desirable style and behaviour. Behaviour speaks louder than words. People are influenced by what they experience rather than what they are told to develop voluntary interest and commitment for organizational success.

(iii) Setting Standards: Quite close to modeling is the setting of standards or norms in the organization, like, standards of individual excellence, mutual support, creativity, innovation and concern for each other. High standards and norms inspire individual employees to follow them in their own work. Leaders are highly motivated persons who strive for their work force /followers and set high standards of performance for themselves and act in a way that provides followers with satisfaction.

(iv) Building Culture and Climate: Senior managers pay major attention to building climate of excellence, commitment, mutual support, etc. They encourage analysis of various organizational

practices, and pay attention to mechanisms, practices, and events etc., that help to evolve a distinct culture for the organization.

(v) Boundary Management: The important function of top leaders is to create conditions conducive to better performance by various groups. This can be done by ensuring continuous availability of resources, supports from outside and from major customers. These external affairs roles, called boundary management, are more important for top management than internal roles pertaining to management of the business. Boundary management also includes developing a strong lobby and interlinkages for the organization.

(vi) Synergising: The strength of an organization depends on the strength of its teams. Team building is one of the very important roles of management.

Searching and Nurturing Talent. Competent, committed individuals with a larger vision are the ultimate strength of an organization. Top management must see this as one of their main functions. Senior managers pay attention to serve as mentor for the organizational employees.

ESTABLISHED THEORIES OF LEADERSHIP

Before analyzing the current status of leadership research, it is important to look at the theoretical development that has occurred through the years. Several approaches to the study of leadership have been adopted and various theories and models developed.

Each of these theories/models has its own contributions, limitations, assumptions, and framework of analysis.

Trait Theory

The earliest trait theories, which can be traced back to the ancient Greeks and Romans, concluded that leaders are born, not made. The "great man" theory of leadership said that a person is born either with or without the necessary traits for leadership. Famous figures in history for example, Napoleon, were said to have had the "natural" leadership abilities to rise out of any situation and become great leaders. The media have long been believers in trait theories of leadership. They identify people such as Margaret Thatcher, Nelson Mandela, Virgin Group CEO Richard Branson, Apple co-founder Steve Jobs, Birla, Tata, Modi etc., as leaders and then describe them in terms such as charismatic, enthusiastic and courageous. The search for personality, social, physical or intellectual attributes that would describe leaders and differentiate them from non - leaders goes back to the 1930s.

Trait is defined as relatively enduring quality of an individual. Various research studies have given intelligence, attitudes, and personality and biological factors as ingredients for effective leaders. **Stogdill** (1948) has presented a review of various research studies. According to him, various trait theories have suggested these traits in a successful leader:

(i) Physical and constitutional factors (height, weight, physique, energy, health, appearance),

(ii) Intelligence and scholarship,

(iii) Personality (self confidence, honesty, integrity, creativity and initiative)

(iv) Sociability and experience,

(v) Will (initiative, persistence, ambition, task orientation),

(*vi*) Dominance and

(*vii*) Surgency (talkative, cheerfulness, geniality, enthusiasm, expressiveness, alertness and originality). In a later study, **Ghiselli** (1971) has found supervisory ability, (management ability, team builder), achievement, motivation, self-actualizing, intelligence, self-confidence, and decisiveness as the qualities related with leadership success.

A review of 20 different studies identified nearly 80 leadership traits. The current research on leadership traits suggests that some factors do help differentiate leaders from non-leaders. The most important traits are a high level of personal drive, desire to lead, personal integrity, and self-confidence, cognitive (analytical) ability, business knowledge, charisma, creativity, flexibility, ambition and energy, honesty, intelligence, and job-relevant knowledge and personal warmth's are also frequently desired. Anderson consulting (a management consultancy firm) conducted (1999) a study on global chief executives to find out the qualities required for an ideal chief executive in the present era of globalised economy. The study highlighted 14 qualities. Accordingly, a chief executive thinks globally, anticipates opportunity, creates a shared vision, develops and empowers people, appreciates cultural diversity, builds teamwork and partnership, empowers people, encourages constructive challenge, ensures customer satisfaction, achieves a competitive advantage, demonstrates personal mastery, shares leadership, and lives the values.

The various studies show wide variations in leadership traits. The various traits can be classified into innate and acquirable traits, on the basis of their source.

Innate qualities are those, which are possessed by various individuals since their birth. These qualities are natural and often known as God-gifted. On the basis of such qualities, it is said that 'leaders are born and not made'. The following are the major innate qualities—physical features, intelligence.

Acquirable qualities of leadership are those, which can be acquired and increased through various processes. Many of these traits can be increased through training and development programmes. Following are the major qualities essential for leadership—emotional stability, human relations, empathy and objectivity, motivating skills, technical skills, communicative skills and social skills.

Limitations

Generalization of traits for a successful leader is not possible. There are no universal traits that predict leadership in all situations; rather, traits appear to predict leadership in selective situations. This was evident by various researches conducted on leadership traits.

Traits predict behaviour more in "weak" situations than in "strong" situations. The evidence is unclear in separating cause from effect. No evidence has been given about the degree of the various traits because people have various traits with different degrees. There is a problem of measuring the traits.

Finally, traits do a better job at predicting the appearance of leadership than in actually distinguishing between effective and ineffective leaders. These situational variables are not incorporated in trait theory.

These limitations have led researchers to look in other directions. Leadership research from the late 1940s through the mid 1960s emphasized the preferred behavioural styles that leaders demonstrated. Under the influence of the behaviourist, school of psychological thought and researchers accepted the fact that leadership traits are not completely inborn but can also be acquired through learning and experience.

Behavioural Theory

Behavioural theory of leadership emphasizes that strong leadership is the result of effective role behaviour and acts, than of its traits. Researchers exploring leadership role wondered if there was something unique in the way that effective leaders behave and came to the conclusion that to operate effectively, leaders have to perform two major functions: Task-related functions (problem solving functions, relate to providing solutions to the problems faced by the groups) and Group maintenance functions (social functions, relate to actions of mediating disputes and ensuring that individuals feel valued by the group). Leadership behaviour was viewed in two ways: functional and dysfunctional. Functional behaviour influenced followers positively (included, setting clear goals, motivating employees for achieving goals, raising the level of morale, building team spirit, effective two-way communication, etc.). Dysfunctional behaviour was unfavorable to the followers (denotes ineffective leadership, such as inability to accept employees ideas, display of emotional immaturity, poor human relations etc.).

Leadership Styles

The behavioural theorists contend that a leader's style is oriented toward either an employee-centered or a job-centered emphasis. In the employee-centered orientation, the leader emphasizes developing friendly, open relationships with employees and is very sensitive to their personal and social needs. A job-centered orientation is one in which the leader emphasizes getting the job done by planning, organizing, delegating, making decisions, evaluating performance, and exercising close management control. Several research efforts have focused on these two extremes and in between levels of leadership behaviour.

Leadership styles are the patterns of behaviour, which a leader adopts in influencing the behaviour of his subordinates in the organizations. These patterns emerge in the leader as he begins to respond in the same fashion under similar conditions and develops habits of actions that become somewhat predictable to those who work with him. Various researchers have proposed different leadership styles. These styles are either based on behavioural approach or situational approach of leadership. Some of the important theories/models prescribing leadership styles are given below.

Leaders' behaviour is affected by two variables leader's characteristics and his hierarchical position in organization.

Based on behavioural approach—

Power orientation leadership as a continuum employee-production orientation, Likert's management system, managerial grid, Tri-dimensional grid etc., are their popular models.

Based on situational approach—

Fiedler's contingency model, Hersey and Blanchard's situational model, Path-goal model etc., are popular models.

Such a classification does not necessarily mean that a particular theory or model grouped under one particular approach of leadership which does not consider the tenets of the other approach.

Limitations

This theory suffers from some basic limitations. First, a particular behaviour may be functional at a point of time but it may be dysfunctional at another point of time. Second, effectiveness of leadership behaviour depends on various factors that are not in the leader but external to him like nature of followers (subordinates) and the situations under which the leader's behaviour takes place, to that extent, the theory does not explain leadership phenomenon fully.

The Iowa Leadership Studies/Leader Continuum: Functional Theory

A series of pioneering leadership studies conducted in the late 1930s by **Ronald Lippitt** and **Ralph K. White** under the general direction of **Kurt Lewin** at the University of Iowa have had a lasting impact, a continuum theory of leadership that identified three basic styles of leadership. At one end of the spectrum is the autocrat, the authoritarian leader, was very directive and allowed no participation. This leader tended to give individual attention when praising and criticizing but tried to be friendly or impersonal rather than openly hostile. The democratic leader encouraged group discussion and decision-making. He tried to be "objective" in his praise or criticism and to be one among the group in spirit. At the other end of the continuum is the laissez-faire leader who gave complete freedom to the group, he essentially provided no leadership.

The research suggested that the democratic leadership style is most effective and productive. It results in a continuous flow of new ideas and positive changes, a sense of group responsibility, and improved quality and quantity of work.

Robert McMurry described the benevolent autocrat as a leader who listens carefully to followers, gives the impression of being democratic, but always makes his or her own personal decision. He argues that the democratic leadership style is too slow and unworkable in our fast-moving business world. A benevolent autocrat is powerful, prestigious, and respected therefore able to move faster and more effectively in a firm.

Limitations

Nevertheless, these leadership studies have extremely important historical significance, sweeping generalizations on the basis of the Lippitt and White studies are not possible. Furthermore, from the viewpoint of modern behavioural science research methodology, many of the variables were not controlled.

Power Orientation in Functioning

Power orientation approach of leadership styles is based on the degree of authority, which a leader uses in influencing the behaviour of his subordinates. Based on the degree of use of power, three types of leadership emerged, as cited below.

Autocratic Leadership

Is also known as authoritarian, directive or monothetic leadership. In this style, a manager centralizes decision-making power in him. He structures the complete situation for his employees and they do what they are told. Here the leadership may be negative because followers are uninformed, insecure, and afraid of leader's authority. There are three categories of autocratic leaders.

(i) ***Strict Autocrat:*** He follows autocratic styles in a very strict sense. His method of influencing subordinates behaviour is through negative motivation, which is by criticizing subordinates, imposing penalty etc.

(ii) ***Benevolent Autocrat:*** He also centralizes decision-making power in him, but his motivation style is positive. He can be effective in getting efficiency in many situations. Some people like to work under strong authority structure and they derive satisfaction by this leadership.

(iii) ***Incompetent Autocrat:*** Sometimes, managers adopt this style just to hide their in competency. However, this cannot be used for a long time.

Limitations

People in the organization dislike this type of leadership, specially when it is strict and the motivational style is negative. Employees lack motivation. Frustration, low morale, and conflict develop in the organization jeopardizing the organizational efficiency. There is more dependence and less individuality in the organization, as such, future leaders in the organization do not develop.

Participative Style

This style is also called democratic, consultative or ideographic. A participative manager decentralizes his decision-making process; he emphasizes consultation and participation of his subordinates. Subordinates are broadly informed about the conditions affecting them and their jobs. The participation may be either real or pseudo. In the case of former, a superior gives credit to subordinates suggestions and ideas in taking the decisions while in the case of latter, the superior preaches participation in theory, but really he does not prefer it in practice. There are various benefits in real participative management. It is a highly motivating technique to employees, as they feel elevated when their ideas and suggestions are given weight in decision-making. The employee's productivity is high, they share the responsibility. It provides organizational stability by raising morale and attitudes of employees high and favourable. Further, leaders are also prepared to take organizational positions. Keeping in view these advantages, management makes attempts for effective participation.

Limitations

The Complex nature of organization requires a thorough understanding of its problems which lower level employees may not be able to do. As such, participation does not remain meaningful at the bottom level.

Free Rein

Free rein or laissez-faire style means giving complete freedom to subordinates. In this style, manager once determines policy, programmes and limitations for action and the entire process is left to subordinates. Group members perform everything and the manager usually maintains contacts with outside persons to bring the information and materials, which the group needs. This helps subordinates to develop independent personality.

Limitations

The contribution of manager is almost nil. It tends to permit different units of an organization to proceed at cross-purposes and can degenerate into chaos. Hence, this style is used very rarely in business organizations.

STRUCTURAL THEORIES

The Ohio State Leadership Studies

Following world war ll the most comprehensive behavioural theories resulted from research that began at Ohio State University in the late 1940s. An interdisciplinary team of researchers analyzed leadership in numerous types of groups and situations like airforce commanders and members of bomber crews, officers, noncommissioned personnel and civilian administrators in the navy department, manufacturing supervisors, executives of regional cooperatives, college administrators, teachers, principals, and school superintendents and leaders of various student and civilian groups and identified two major dimensions of leader behaviour: Initiating structure and Consideration. Initiating structure is the degree to which leaders are concerned with organizational structure, definition of the jobs to be done, pressure for work output, defining communication channels, and evaluation of group output. Consideration involves the leaders concern for mutual trust, satisfaction, and well being of employees, respectful relationship, employee support, approachability, and effective communication. Extensive research, found that leaders high in initiating structure and consideration tended to achieve high employee performance and satisfaction more frequently than those who rated low on either dimension or both.

Limitations

Studies indicated that high style on both the dimensions did not always result in positive consequences as enough exceptions were found to indicate that situational factors needed to be integrated into the theory. Other studies found that high consideration was negatively related to performance ratings of the leader by his superior and also that no single style was the most effective in all instances.

University of Michigan Studies

Leadership studies undertaken at the University of Michigan's Survey Research Center, at about the same time as those is being done at Ohio State, had similar research objectives to locate behavioural characteristics of leaders that appeared to be related to measures of performance effectiveness. The Michigan group also came up with two dimensions of leadership behaviour that they labelled as employee oriented and production oriented. Leaders who were employee oriented were described as emphasizing interpersonal relations; they took personal interest in the needs of their employees and accepted individual differences among members. The production-oriented leaders, in contrast, tended to emphasize the technical or task aspects of the job- their main concern was in accomplishing their group's tasks and the group members were the means to that end.

The conclusions arrived at by the Michigan researchers strongly favored the leaders who were employee oriented in their behaviour were associated with higher group productivity and higher job satisfaction. Production-oriented leaders tended to be associated with low group productivity and lower job satisfaction.

Limitations

Sometime overlooked, finding, that employee satisfaction was not directly related to productivity.

FUNCTIONAL MODELS

The Managerial Grid

One very popular functional model was developed by **Blake & Mouton** to identify leadership styles, known as managerial grid. It depicts two dimensions: Concern for Production and Concern for People. The five basic styles identified in the grid represent varying combinations of concern for people (people includes degree of personal commitment toward goal achievement, maintaining the self-esteem to workers, responsibility based on trust, and satisfying inter-personal relations.) and concern for production (attitudes of superiors towards quality of policy decisions, procedures and processes, creativeness of research, quality of staff services, work efficiency and volume of output).

Blake and Mouton plotted five major leadership style:

1. Little concern for either production or people. (The impoverished type, worst leadership style.)
2. Lowest concern for production, highest for people. (The country-club type, people-oriented style.)
3. Highest concern for production, lowest for people. (The autocrat type, production-oriented style.)
4. Comfortable concern for both production and people. (The middle-of-the-road type, maintain present balance style.)
5. Highest concern for both production and people. (The team type, peak of leadership styles.)

Limitations

It does not tell why a manager falls in one part or the other of the grid. What type of manager's style will be when influenced by factors like, the superior, the kind of subordinates he supervises, and the situation in which he finds himself.

There is little substantive evidence to support the conclusion that a team type style is most effective in all situations.

DEVELOPMENT ORIENTED MODEL

Scandinavian Studies

Scandinavian researchers in Finland and Sweden have been conducting new studies to reassess whether there are only two dimensions that capture the essence of leadership behaviour. Their basic premise is that in a changing world, effective leaders would exhibit development-oriented behaviour. These are leaders who value experimentation seek new ideas and generate and implement change. Researchers have found strong support for development-oriented leader behaviour as a separate and independent dimension. It also appears that leaders who demonstrate development-oriented behaviour have more satisfied employees and is seen as more competent by those employees.

Limitations

Initial conclusions need to be guarded, without more confirming evidence.

Model of Likert's Management System

Rensis Likert and his associates of University of Michigan, USA, have studied four styles of leadership, called systems of management leadership from an Employee-centered and Job-centered perspective and concluded: "Supervisors with the best records of performance focus their primary attention on the human aspects of their subordinates problems and on endeavoring to build effective work groups with high performance goals. These styles may be referred to as exploitative autocrat- system1 (here the manager is very authoritarian and exploitative.), benevolent autocrat-system 2 (here manager keeps strict control but also values the interest of employees.), participative-system 3 (here the approach is consultative but final decision remains with manager.) and democratic- system 4 (this is a participative management style and decisions are made by consensus and majority.). Likert on the basis of intensive research has shown that high producing departments in several organizational studies are marked by system 4 (democratic).

Each leadership style or system is defined by at least seven operating characteristics, which include: Character of motivational forces, communication process, interaction-influence process, decision-making process, goal setting or, control processes and performance characteristics.

Limitations

There is no universality of the systems, hence more observation is required.

Model of Tridimensional Grid

Reddin conceptualized a three-dimensional grid, also known as 3-D model, borrowing some of the ideas from managerial grid. Three-dimensional axes represent task-orientation (extent to which a manager directs his subordinates efforts towards goal attainment by planning, organizing, and controlling), relationship orientation (the extent to which a manager has personal relationships characterized by mutual trust, respect for subordinates ideas and suggestions and their feelings) and effectiveness orientation (extent to which a manager is successful and effective in his position and a given situation). By adding an effectiveness dimension, the concepts of leadership styles with the situational demand has been integrated by them. This has given birth to four basic types of leaders/managers.

The separated manager is concerned with correcting deviations. He writes rules and policies and enforces them. The related manager accepts others as he finds them, does not worry about time, sees the organization as a social system, likes to work with others and obtains co-operation of others by setting examples. The dedicated manager is domineering, interested only in production and does not identify with subordinates. He cannot work without power. The integrated manager gets himself and his people involved with organization. There is free two-way communication and strong identification and emphasis on teamwork. Thus, the four basic managerial styles results into eight less and more effective styles as follows.

Ineffective styles are: Deserter (has both low task and low people orientation), Missionary (shows only interest in harmony, and does not take initiative). Autocrat (concerned with authority, his decisions are unilateral and centralized and relies more on negative motivation). Compromiser (uses a high task and relationship orientation, is a poor decision maker and, allows various pressures in the situation to influence him).

The four corresponding effective styles are as follows.

1. *Bureaucrat:* Has high orientation towards organizational rules and regulations, less task and relationship-oriented produces only few ideas and does not take initiative.

2. *Developer:* Tends to display implicit trust in people relies on high relationship orientation and less task orientation believes in commitment to work, openness, freedom to act, self-expression, and development of subordinates.

3. *Benevolent Autocrat:* Directive manager who knows what he wants and often gets it without creating resentment is high task and less people oriented adopts positive economic motivation for getting things done and follows feudalistic approach.

4. *Executive:* Has a high task and high relationship orientation in a situation where such behaviour is appropriate emphasizes team management, acts as a powerful motivational instrument in the organization, is democratic leadership style.

Limitations

The three-dimensional model recognizes that a manager may use more than one style and no single style is suggested to be appropriate in all situations.

Situational or Contingency Theories/Models

The situational approach was initially called Zeitgeist (a German word meaning *"spirit of the times"*). The leader is viewed as a product of the times and the situation. Situational leadership approach (also known as contingency theory) was applied for the first time, in 1920 in the armed forces of Germany with the objective to get good generals under different situations. In the business organizations, much emphasis on the leadership researches was placed on the situations that surrounded the exercise of leadership since early 1950s. The organizational situation can include such variables as the climate, managers and subordinates values, attitudes and experience and the nature of the particular work to be accomplished including time and money. Besides, leaders behaviour, characteristics, hierarchical position and situational factors also affect leadership effectiveness. We will examine some of the most popular situational theories that attempt to fulfill this goal.

Fiedler's Contingency Model

Fiedler and his associates were among the first to develop a contingency leadership model, which suggests that leadership styles must fit or match the situation in order to be effective. They described leaders in terms of relationship or task-motivated behaviour. After studying hundreds of organizations and leaders, he concluded that leadership style effectiveness depends on the interaction of the leader's motivational behaviour with three situational variables within the organization:

(*i*) leader-member relations (refer to the leader's acceptance by group members),

(*ii*) task structure (concerns how routine and structured a job is), and

(*iii*) leader position power (refers to the legitimate, coercive, and reward power bases from which a leader can operate).

Clarifying these variables, Fiedler developed an eight-cell model, which suggests that the most effective leadership style is based on the combination of the three variables in an organizational work situation. For example, Fiedler contends that if leader-member relations are good in a very structured task setting and the leader's position power is strong, then a task-oriented leadership style would be most effective. However, if relations are good but task structure is not routine and position power is weak, a relation-oriented style is most successful.

Limitations

Contingency variables are complex to understand like it is often difficult to determine, how good the leader-member relations are, how structured the task is, and how much position power the leader has and how a perfect match can be made between these variables? Moreover, no leadership style is appropriate for all situations.

Cognitive Resource Theory

More recently, Fiedler and an associate, Joe Garcia, reconceptualized the former original theory. Specially, they have focused on the role of stress as a form of situational unfavorableness and how a leader's intelligence and experience influence his or her reaction to stress. They called this reconceptualisation as cognitive resource theory.

The essence of the new theory is that *stress is the enemy of rationality*. It's difficult for leaders to think logically and analytically when they are under stress. Moreover, the importance of a leader's intelligence and experience to his or her effectiveness differs under low and high stress situations. Basically, Fiedler and Garcia found that intelligence and experience interfere with each other. This has led to three conclusions:

1. Directive behaviour results in good performance only if linked with high intelligence in supportive low-stress situations
2. In high-stress situations, there is a positive relationship between job experience and performance and

3. The intellectual abilities of leaders correlate with group performance in situations where leader perceives as low in stress.

Limitations

Inspite of its newness, cognitive resource theory requires a solid body of research support.

Heresy and Blanchard's Situational Model

Paul Hersey and Ken Blanchard have developed a leadership model called Situational Leadership Theory (SLT) that has gained a strong followings among management development and training programs. The model identifies two major styles: *Task style* (related with organizing and defining task for subordinate) and *Relationship style* (the leader has close personal relations with subordinates, there is an open communication and psychological support). In this model, the emphasis on the followers in leadership effectiveness reflects the reality that it is the follower who accept or reject the leader regardless of what the leader does. This is an important dimension that has been overlooked in most leadership theories. The term readiness, as defined by **Hersey** and **Blanchard**, refers to the extent to which people have the ability and willingness to accomplish a specific task. Accordingly they incorporated the maturity of the followers into their model. The level of maturity is defined by three criteria: degree of achievement motivation, willingness to take on responsibility and amount of education or experience. The key for leadership effectiveness in this model is to match up the situation according to the need of maturity of subordinates with the appropriate style, which moves in stages and has a cycle; hence this theory is also known as Life-cycle theory of leadership. The following summarizes the four basic styles:

(*i*) *Telling style:* This is a high –task, low-relationship style and is effective when followers are at a very low level of maturity.

(*ii*) *Selling style:* This is a high–task, high-relationship style and is effective when followers are on the low level of maturity.

(*iii*) *Participating style:* This is a low–task, high-relationship style and is effective when followers are on the high level of maturity.

(*iv*) *Delegating style:* This is a low–task, low-relationship style and is effective when followers are at a very high level of maturity.

Limitations

This approach has limited utility for identifying leadership effectiveness, besides there has not been much research evidence to support the applicability of the model. Possible explanations include internal ambiguities and inconsistencies in the model itself as well as problems with research methodology in tests of the theory.

Leadership as a Continuum

Tannenbaum and **Schmidt** (1973) have depicted a broad range of styles on a continuum moving from authoritarian leadership behaviour at one end to free-rein behaviour at the other end. Neither extreme is absolute and authority, and freedom are never without their limitations. It depends upon three factors: Forces in manager, Forces in subordinate and Forces in situation. This new continuum of leadership pattern is more complex and dynamic, reflecting the organizational and social realities than the previous one. Here the total area of freedom shared by the manager and non- manager is constantly redefined by interaction between them and the forces in environment. A successful leader is one who is keenly aware of those forces, which are more relevant to his behaviour at any given time.

Limitations

Merely understanding these forces correctly is not enough but leader can be successful only when he is able to behave appropriately in the light of these perceptions and understanding.

Group and Exchange Model of Leadership

The group theories of leadership have their roots in social psychology. There must be a positive exchange between the leaders and followers in order for group goals to be accomplished. More recently, this social exchange view of leadership has been summarized as follows:

Exchange theories propose that group members make contributions at a cost to themselves and receive benefits at a cost to the group or other members. Interaction continues because members find the social exchange mutually rewarding. The above quotation emphasizes that leadership is an exchange process between the leader and followers.

Leader-Member Exchange Theory/The Vertical Dyad Linkage Model

Relevant to the exchange view of leadership is the Vertical Dyad Linkage (VDL) approach more recently called Leader Member Exchange (LMX). In particular, leaders and subordinates develop dyadic (two person) relationships, which affect the behaviour of both leaders and subordinates.

The Leader-Member exchange (LMX) theory argues that because of time pressures, leaders establish a special relationship with a small group of their followers. These individuals make up the in-group upon which they are trusted, get a disproportionate amount of leader's attention, and are more likely to receive special privileges. Other followers fall into the out-group as they get less of the leader's time, fewer of the preferred rewards that the leader controls, and have leader follower relations based on formal authority interactions. A key point to note here is, that even though it is the leader who is making the choice, it is the follower's characteristics that are driving the leaders categorizing decision.

Research to test LMX theory has been very supportive. However, at present VDL or LMX seems to be more descriptive of the typical process of role making by leaders, rather than prescribing the pattern of exchange relations optimal for leadership effectiveness.

Limitations

The theory lacks empirical support and many research findings have given contradictory outcomes.

Path Goal Theory/Model

Currently, one of the most respected models of leadership is the path goal model, developed by **Robert House.** Path goal theory is a contingency model of leadership that extracts key elements from leadership research on Initiating structure and Consideration and the Expectancy theory of motivation.

The essence of the path goal theory is that it's the leaders job to assist followers in attaining their goals and clarifying the path, by providing the necessary direction and support.

House identified four leadership behaviours. The directive leader lets followers know what is expected of them, schedules work to be done, and gives specific guidance as to how to accomplish tasks. The supportive leader is friendly and shows concern for the needs of followers. The participative leader consults with followers and uses their suggestions before making a decision. The achievement oriented leader sets challenging goals and expects followers to perform at their highest level. House assumes leaders are flexible and that the same leader can display any or all of these behaviours depending on the situation.

The model proposes two classes of situational or contingency variables that moderate the leadership behaviour outcome relationship those in the environment that are outside the control of the employee (task structure, the formal authority system, and the work group) and those that are part of the personal characteristics of the employee (locus of control, experience and perceived ability). Environmental factors determine the type of leader behaviour required as a complement if follower outcomes are to be maximized while personal characteristics of the employee determine how the environment and leader behaviour are interpreted. The research evidence generally supports the logic underlying the path-goal theory *i.e.,* employee performance and satisfaction are likely to be positively influenced when the leader compensates for things lacking in either the employee or the work setting. However, the leader who spends time explaining tasks when those tasks are already clear or when the employee has the ability and experience to handle them without interference is likely to be ineffective because the employee will see such directive behaviour as redundant.

Limitations

The theory lacks empirical support and many research findings have given contrasting results.

Leadership Decision Theory/Leader Participation Model/Vroom-Yetton Leadership Model

In 1973, **Victor Vroom** and **Phillip Yetton** researched on leadership style in the context of how much participation the leader should allow subordinates in making decisions. They identify five leadership styles, seven situation dimensions, fourteen problem types, and seven decision rules, based on the degree of employee participation and power in making organizational decisions.

Autocrative I: This style recommends that the leader solve all the problems and individually make a decision using information available at the time of the decision.

Autocrative II: This style recommends that the leader obtain necessary information from subordinates and then personally make the decision without involving subordinates.

Consultive I: This style suggests that the leader share information concerning the problem with subordinates individually, solicit and obtain suggestions from subordinates.

Consultive II: This style recommends that the leader share problems with subordinates as a collective group obtain ideas and suggestions from the group and then personally make a decision.

Group: This style suggests that the leader share the problem with the entire group and together generate and evaluate alternatives in an attempt to reach a consensus solution to the problem.

The Vroom-Yetton model suggests that seven questions must be answered to determine the most appropriate leadership style for any given managerial decision. Vroom and Yetton developed a decision tree model that allows an individual to determine what leadership style is most appropriate based on the answers to these questions. The best style is contingent upon changing factors in the decision-making and problem-solving situations within the organization. More recent work by Vroom and Arthur Jago has resulted in revision of this model. The new model retains the same five alternative leadership styles but adds a set of problem types and expands the contingency variables to twelve.

Limitations

Other contingency theories demonstrate that stress, intelligence and experience are important situational variables. Yet the leader participation model fails to include them. Then the model is far too complicated for the typical manager to use on a regular basis. While Vroom and Jago have developed a program to guide mangers in the revised model, it's not very realistic to expect practicing mangers to consider twelve contingency variables, eight problem types and five leadership styles in trying to select the appropriate decision process for a specific problem.

Neocharismatic Theories: Emerging Theoretical Frameworks for Leadership

The final set of leadership model emerged has been called Neocharismatic theories/ model. It has three common themes. First, it stresses symbolic and emotionally appealing leader's behaviour. Second, it attempts to explain how certain leaders are able to achieve extraordinary levels of follower commitment. And third, it de-emphasizes theoretical complexity and looks at leadership more the way the average "person on the street" today views.

Charismatic Concept of Leadership

Although the charismatic concept or charisma goes as far back as the ancient Greeks and is cited in the Bible, its modern development is attributed to the work of Robert House. Charismatic leadership theory depicts a leader having some charisma which acts as influencer. Charisma is a Greek word—meaning *gift*. Thus, charisma is a God-gifted attribute in a person, which makes him a leader—irrespective of the situations in which he works. Because of the effects that charismatic leaders have on followers, the theory predicts that charismatic leaders will produce in follower's performance beyond expectations as well as strong commitment to the leader and his mission.

Charismatic leadership theory says that followers make attributions of heroic or extraordinary leadership abilities when they observe certain behaviours. There have been a number of studies that have attempted to identify personal characteristics of the charismatic leader. The best documented study has isolated five such characteristics—charismatic leaders have a vision, are willing to take risks to achieve that vision, are sensitive to both environmental constraints and follower needs and exhibit behaviours that are out of the ordinary that differentiate charismatic leaders form non-charismatic ones.

Transformational and Transactional Theories of Leadership

Most of the leadership theories and models presented are concerned with transactional leaders. These kinds of leaders guide and motivate their followers in the direction of established goals by clarifying role and task requirements. There is also another type of leader who inspires followers to transcend their own self-interests for the good of the organization and who is capable of having a profound and extraordinary effect on his followers, these are transformational leaders. They pay attention to the concerns and developmental needs of individual followers, they change followers awareness of issues by helping them to look at old problems in new ways and they are able to excite, arouse, and inspire followers to put out extra effort to achieve group goals.

Concept of Actualization of Roles

Conceptual Framework of Role

Role is the position one occupies in a social system, and is defined by the functions one performs in response to the expectations of the significant members of a social system, and one's own expectations from that position or office.

Role and office/position are separate concepts, though two side of the same coin. According to **Katz** and **Kahn**, office is essentially a relational concept, defining each position in terms of its relationships to others and to the system as a whole, while role is an obligational concept. A role is not defined without the expectations of the role senders, including the role occupant.

The concept of role is vital for the integration of the individual with an organization. The organization has its own structure and goals; similarly, the individual has his personality and needs. Role is also a central concept in work motivation as it is only through this, that the individual and organization interact with each other.

The concept of role widens the meaning of work and the relationships of the worker with other significant persons in the system. The concept of job is more prescriptive relationship of the worker with his supervisor whereas the role emphasizes his relationship with all those who have expectation from him. Recently, much emphasis has been given to the development of roles and making them more effective in an organization.

The Concept of Role-Efficacy

The concept of Role-Efficacy was originally initiated by **Kahn & Associates** (1964). According to **Pareek** (1987), when an individual joins an organization he is appraised of the duties he has to perform. At the same time, he projects his own expectations from the role. The performance of a person working in an organization depends on his own potential effectiveness as a person, his technical competence, his managerial experience, etc., as well as the way the role which he performs in the organization is designed. It is the integration of the two (the person and the role) that ensures the person's effectiveness in the organization. Competency is the primary resources that need to be built. Unless a person has the requisite knowledge, technical competence and skills required for the role, he will not be effective. Equally important is how the role, which he occupies in the organization, is designed. If the role does not allow the person to use his competence, and if he constantly feels frustrated in the role, his effectiveness is likely to be low. The integration of a person and a role comes about when the latter is able to fulfill the needs of the individual, and when the individual in turn is able to contribute to the evolution of the role.

Effectiveness of a person-in–a-role-in-an- organization, therefore, may depend on his own potential effectiveness, the potential effectiveness of the role and the organizational climate. The potential effectiveness can be called efficacy. Personal efficacy would mean potential effectiveness of a person in personal and interpersonal situations.

Role efficacy would mean the potential effectiveness of an individual occupying a particular role in an organization, as he perceives it in the constellation of various significant roles appropriately called, role-set. Role efficacy can be seen as the psychological factor underlying role effectiveness. In short, role efficacy is potential effectiveness of a role.

It is also important how the individual gives his personal meanings to the various sets of expectations from the organization and various sets of facilities/difficulties, authorities/duties given by the organization to him in the context of his personal potential, skill, competency, values, needs, and personal expectations. This mental process of giving meaning is called Role-perception. If he gives positive meaning, it is called positive perception and if he gives negative meaning, it is called negative perception (**Pandey**, 1997).

The concept of Role-efficacy purports to generate a feeling of pleasantness in performing one's role and meeting the demands of the role. Perhaps in the context of great challenges being faced by the organizations, the concept of role-efficacy has got potential to bring about a change in the work culture.

Aspects of Role-Efficacy

Aspects of role efficacy are classified into three groups. One dimension is **role making** (as opposed to role taking), the former is an active attitude towards defining and making one's role as one likes, a healthy climate, which empowers people is generally a reliable source for inferring the degree of role making behaviour of various functionaries, whereas the latter is a passive attitude that mainly responds to other's expectations. The second dimension is concerned with increasing the power of the role making. This is called as **role centering**, which can be contrasted with role entering (accepting the role as given and reconciling oneself to its present importance or unimportance). The third dimension is called **role linking** (extending, the relationship of the role with other roles and groups) contrasted with role shrinking (making the role narrow, confined to the work related expectations).

Role-Making

Self-role Integration (Vs. Role Distance)

The dimension measures the perception of the integration between self and role. The integration of the person and the role comes about when the individual is able to contribute to the evolution of the role. Every person has strengths, experience, technical training, special skills, and some unique contribution to make. When his role provides him with greater opportunity for using such special strengths, his role efficacy is likely to be higher. This is called self-role integration. On the other hand, if there is a distance between the self and the role, role efficacy is likely to be low.

Proactivty (Vs. Reacting)

The dimension measures the perception of taking initiative. A person who occupies a role responds to the various expectations that people in the organization have from that role, while this certainly gives him satisfaction; it also satisfies others in the organization. However, if he is also expected to take the initiative in starting some activity, the efficacy will be higher. Reactive behaviour (responding to the expectations of others) helps a person to be effective to some extent, but proactivity (taking the initiative rather than only responding to other's expectations) contributes much more to efficacy.

Creativity (Vs. Routinity)

This dimension measures the perception that something new or innovative is being done by the individual i.e., experimenting and trying new ideas and strategies. If a person perceives that he has to perform only routine tasks, it becomes detrimental for high role efficacy. If he feels that the role does not allow any time or opportunity to be creative and to try out new and unconventional ways of solving problems, efficacy is bound to be low.

Confrontation (Vs. Avoidance)

This dimension measures the perception about the capacity of the individual to face the problems to attempt their relevant solution. In general, if people in an organization avoid problems or shift them on to others, their role efficacy will be low. The tendency to confront problems contributes to high efficacy.

Role Centering (Contrasted with Role Entering)

Centrality (Vs. Peripherality)

This dimension measures the perception of importance of the role *i.e.*, if a person is feeling his role is important or central in a system his role efficacy is likely to be high. If people feel that their roles are peripheral *i.e.*, not very important, their potential effectiveness will be low as higher motivation is directly proportional to the importance of the roles.

Influence (Vs. Powerlessness)

A relative concept is that of influence or power. This dimension measures the perception of the individuals towards one's own capacity in making an impact on others. The more influence a person is able to exercise in his role, the higher his efficacy is likely to be.

Growth (Vs. Stagnation)

This dimension measures the perception about on occupying a role the level of opportunities to learn new things for personal growth and development. If a person feels that his role is stagnant without any opportunity to grow, he is likely to have low role efficacy.

Role-linking (Contrasted with Role–Shrinking)

Inter-role Linkage (Vs. Isolation)

This dimension measures the perception of inter dependence with others role *i.e.*, linkage of one's roles with other's role. Linking one's role with others in the organization increases efficacy.

Helping Relationship (Vs. Hostility)

This dimension measures the perception/feeling of a person with regard to helping other and taking help from others. If person performing a particular role feels that he can get help from some source in the organization whenever the need arises, he is likely to have higher role efficacy.

Super Ordination (Vs. Deprivation)

This dimension measures the perception that something beyond the regular call of duty is being contributed to larger society and the nation *i.e.*, linkage of one's role with larger entity/ cause. When a person performing a particular role feels that what he does is likely to be of value to a larger group, his efficacy is likely to be high.

Review of Research in Regard to Role-Efficacy

Much research has been done on role-efficacy and organizational dimensions. The concept of Role-Efficacy has its roots in the role theory, enunciating the idea that people do have multiple roles and in an organization, they relate through a role specific activity, expectations and goal attainment (**Sarbin & Allen**, 1975; **Pareek**, 1987). The several constituent elements of organizational effectiveness identified by **Cameron** and **Whetton** (1983), place heavy demands on organizational roles.

Attempts at role-efficacy construct definition through survey data have been made by several researchers (**Sen**, 1982; **Surti**, 1983; **Sayeed**, 1992). These can be recognized as meaningful insofar as the development of role efficacy measure is concerned.

Cattell's three contact personality factors were found to have significant positive correlation with role-efficacy. *Viz. cyclothemia* (broadly speaking people – orientation), *surgence* (broadly speaking- extraversion), and *adventurous* (broadly speaking -outgoing tendency).

On the personal side, role-efficacy has been reported to have high and positive correlation with internal locus of control. There is positive and significant correlation between role efficacy and internality, and significant negative correlation with externality of all kinds (relating to others, relating to chance and the total). It seems persons with high role efficacy have higher belief in influencing the outcomes relevant to them, and vice versa.

Surti, found negative correlation between role-efficacy and dominance. Study also revealed negative correlation between role-efficacy and Machiavellianism.

Research on role-efficacy indicates that persons with high role-efficacy experience less role stress (Sen, 1982; Surti, 1983), less anxiety (Deo, 1993), less work related tension (Sayeed, 1985), less other different types of stresses (Pestonjee and Pandey, 1996) and feel more satisfied with life in general and with their jobs/roles in particular (Pareek, 1993). Sharma and Sharma (1984) attempted to relate role-efficacy with job-anxiety and tension. Role-efficacy was found as effective style for coping with role-stress (Pestonjee 1982).

They rely on their own strengths to effectively cope up with problems (Sen 1982, Surti, 1983), use more purposeful behaviour, (Das, 1984), remain active and interact with people and the environment, show perseverance or higher level of emotional intelligence (Goleman, 1995) and persist in solving problems by themselves and sometimes by taking help of other people, show growth orientation, attitudinal commitment, positive and approach behaviour, (Sen, 1982; Deo 1993) and feel satisfied with their life, jobs and organizational role in general (Sen, 1982; Surti, 1983).

Managerial behaviour was measured in terms of approach (functional) and avoidance (dysfunctional) behaviour on six motivations (*achievement, influence, extension, control, affiliation,* and *dependency*). It was found that approach behaviour scores correlated positively with role efficacy for six motives, avoidance behaviour scores were negatively correlated, when role efficacy scores were correlated with "operating effectiveness" on the six motives, all correlations were found to be positive and significant. It can thus be concluded that persons with high role efficacy tend to use their needs (motives) more effectively during their work in the organization. They tend to show low dysfunctional behaviour, (**Deo** 1993).

Reanalysis of the data (Sen's) showed negative correlation between role-efficacy and a measure of alienation. There was a positive correlation between role-efficacy and job satisfaction. Role satisfaction was measured by a discrepancy measure between perceived and desired levels of satisfaction on five needs (achievement, influence, extension, control, and affiliation). Role-efficacy was found to have positive correlation with general satisfaction and role satisfaction.

The individuals with higher role efficacy use less defensive mechanisms in their interpersonal transactions (**Shingala,** 1985).

Role-efficacy is also positively correlated with the length of service, individual's age, type of roles and location of the work place as it was found that respondent whose offices were located far, perceived their roles as more central and more influential but had lower self – role integration, than those in head quarters, (Moran, 1986; Sen, 1982; Surti, 1983). Personal attributes and job demographics were found to have impact on role - efficacy (Sayeed, 1985b). The same trend was found for proactivity.

Regarding motivational and participative climate of the organization, positive correlation has been reported by Sen. Multi-linkage and team oriented groups had higher mean values consistently on the role-efficacy, dimensions reflecting such inclination on the part of employees that contribute to personal efficacy and account for participative orientation of the person concerned (Sayeed, 1995). On the other hand, a climate characterized by control and affiliation seems to lower employees role-efficacy (Sen, 1982; Pareek, 1982; Surti, 1983). Innovation fostering climate was also found to be a strong predictor of role-efficacy dimensions (Deo, 1993). Role-efficacy has also been reported as a strong moderator variable, which accounted for systematic influence in predicting or enhancing the effect on organizational climate and other organization related measures (**Das,** 1984; **Sayeed,** 1992).

To sum up, a participative climate in which the employees get higher job satisfaction, contributes to role-efficacy. It seems that the climate promoting concern for excellence, innovation, the quality of work life (measured by influence, amenities at the work place, nature of job, and supervisory behaviour, availability of learning opportunity on the job, variety in work, challenge in the job, and leisure time recreation, age, and influence, use of expertise, and concern for the larger issues also contributes to role efficacy **Gupta** and **Khandelwal,** 1988). They concluded that high role-efficacy and excellent quality of work life are required to ensure the highest level of productivity on a job.

A worth noting study, conducted by Das (1984) on managers of engineering industry in India, concluded that role-efficacy had an important moderating effect on dependent (purposeful job behaviour) and independent variables (demographic factors, organizational climate, and role stress). The role making behaviour—a complex process is likely to be experienced by the individual if the role incumbent is willing to initiate affirmative action plans, interacts positively with the environment, and makes best use of the feedback from the organizational environment (**Pareek**, 1976; **Sayeed**, 1988).

The concept of role-efficacy in the Indian context has been pioneered by Prof. Pareek (1974, 1975,1976,1978, 1980a, 1980b, 1984, 1986, 1987, and 1993). Pareek's earlier expositions of role-efficacy and also his recent work are based on a deep understanding of role perceptions derived from empirical and action researches, laying emphasis on the normative and development aspects of role which he believes one significant building blocks for integrating individual in an organization (**Argyris**, 1964; **Graen**, 1976). Following him, a number of researchers have endeavored to unfold the relationship of the role-efficacy with personal and organizational variables. If a given organizational role controls the person, the role incumbent is less likely to demonstrate risk taking and judicious handling of things and people, and his/her inner urge for doing things differently or more innovatively also suffers, with the result that the role occupant fails to enjoy the job and slowly tends to succumb to the bindings of the organization. **Allinson** (1984) referred to such adjustments of individuals as a clear demonstration of bureaucratic role orientations, devoid of personal enthusiasm for results. On the contrary, if an individual is able to exercise his personal influence in the role he occupies, and moulds the role he is more likely to expand the role boundaries. Thereby, his role performance might become qualitative more meaningful to himself and the organization alike. **Graen** (1976) referred to such orientations and/or behaviours as role making functions, which individuals are supposed to initiate in the organization.

The role making behaviour—a complex process, is likely to be experienced by the individual if the role incumbent is willing to initiate affirmative actions plans, interacts positively with the environment, and makes best use of the feedback from the organizational environment (Pareek, 1976 Sayeed, 1988). As Nadler (1988) has pointed out, feedback generation within the organization is the key for successful organizational change and development. In the same way, the role making behaviour proves to be a key factor in effective rearrangement and networking of the roles at the micro level of the organization.

Conducive work environment was found to make leadership work which ultimately influenced role-efficacy of organizational members and productivity of organizations (Sayeed 1992a). Strong linkage was found to exist between role-efficacy and appropriate position power structure (Sayeed 1992b).

Role-Efficacy was reported to have some psychological correlation in organizations with information technology (Deo 1993).

Role-Efficacy was also found to bring about a positive change in performance, interpersonal relations and overall job-behaviour of supervisors (Pandey, 1994). Role- efficacy was found to be an effective intervention to prevent accidents (Pandey, 1995,a). Role-efficacy was found to be negatively related with role-stress, (Pandey, 1995, b). Age, qualification, and experience were found to predict role-efficacy in some part (Pandey, 1995, c).

The organizations that are serious in strategic development look forward for enhancing employee's potentialities, to adequately reflect in their role performance. For this purpose, several tools and techniques are used. Some prefer to employ techniques of restructuring organizational systems and procedures, so that the redesigned system could function in a coordinated and efficient manner, whereas others lay heavy emphasis on analyzing the dynamics of the underlying relationships, use of power and authority, conflict handling at superior and subordinate levels (in dyads), the goal setting process and continuous review with or without collateral structural changes.

Still others believe in experimenting with the organizational change process by way of introducing appropriate organizational values (Woodcock and Dave, 1989' Chakraborty, 1992); culture building (Pareek, 1994), enhancing organizational learning (Senge, 1990), and creating a conflict positive organization (Tjsevold, 1993). Even though organizational learning generally takes place with the application of any of the above approaches, strategic development in a given organization is likely to be well attained, if the organization remains activated by a compelling thought process at the top to create and sustain new learning within its fold.

Role-efficacy has been found to be positively correlated with job satisfaction and the perception of a participative climate in one's organizations, and negatively correlated with alienation and anxiety (Pareek, 1993, for a review of these studies).

Pareek (1987–1993) suggested that in the interest of growth and development and for enhancing HRD orientation of the company, organizations need to carry out role efficacy audits in various job-settings and embark upon appropriate strategies to bring about a change in various segments of such perception through performance counseling and utility analysis.

Role-efficacy as a framework for understanding the interactions of individuals with their roles and the process resulting from these interactions have generated greater interest in the last two decades. The concept is equally important for making interventions for organizational development and generating research data for testing the linkages of role behaviour (Pandey, 2001).

According to (Pareek, 2001), organizations have to assist individuals to define their roles and in the process individuals are to be willing to share their concerns for organization through appropriate strategies for organizational development. The primary role of transformational leadership is to multiply power in the organization, build the organization as a learning organization and develop an appropriate culture, ethos and climate.

REVIEW OF RESEARCH IN REGARD TO CORPORATE LEADERSHIP

Although the Oxford English Dictionary (1933) noted the appearance of the word "leader" in the English language as early as the year 1300, the word "leadership" did not appear until the first half of the nineteenth century. Surveys of job satisfaction from the 1920s onward illustrated the importance of leadership.

Characteristics of a transformational leader: **Behling** and **McFillen** (1960) built a model of transformational leadership six attributes of transformational leadership included in the model are discussed as: display empathy, dramatizes the mission, project self-assurance, enhances the leader's image, assures followers of their competency, provides followers with opportunities to experience success.

Many researches have studied (Bennis & Nanus, 1985; Conger & Kanungo, 1978; House, 1977, Kuhnert & Lewis, 1987; Sashkin, 1988; Tichy & Devanna, 1986) behaviour and traits of transformational leaders which includes empathy, need for power, good rhetorical followers to gain their commitment, and make them feel that they are being traded with due respect and dignity. Thus, they reflect the behaviour and traits required for initiating change such as strong analytical and diagnostic skills, a high energy level, a business strategist and risk taker, crisis management skill, and good negotiation skill.

The evidence supporting the superiority of transformational leadership over the transactional variety is overwhelmingly impressive. For instance, a number of studies with U.S., Canadian and

German military officers found at every level that transformational leader were evaluated as more effective than their transactional counterparts, and managers at Federal Express who were rated by their followers as exhibiting more transformational leadership were evaluated by their immediate supervisors as high performers and more promotable. In summary, the overall evidence indicates that transformational leadership is more strongly correlated than transactional leadership with lower turnover rates, higher productivity and higher employee satisfaction.

Most experimental research, unfortunately, has focused on transactional leadership (Hollander, 1978), whereas the real movers and shakers of the world are transformational leaders. Although both types of leaders sense the felt needs of their followers, it is the transformational leader who raises consciousness (about higher considerations) through articulation and role modeling.

Identifying transformational characteristics of leaders can become very important as organizations transform traditional ways of being led to meet the challenge of dramatic change. It is the transformation process that has led to the transformational theory. Transformational leadership occurs when leaders and followers raise one another to higher levels of motivation and morality. Leaders address themselves to follower's wants, needs, and motivation, as well as to their own, and thus any serve as an independent force in changing the makeup of the followers motive by gratifying their motives. Transactional leadership use style and techniques of the kind already described to clarify task requirements and ensures that subordinates are rewarded for appropriate behaviour and performance. Transformational leadership on the other hand, concentrates on articulating a vision and mission, creating and maintaining a positive image in the mind of employees (**Burns**, 1978).

According to the accepted view (**Bass,** 1985) transactional and transformational leadership should not be viewed as opposing approaches to getting things done. Transformational leadership is built on top of transactional leadership; it produces levels of follower effort and performance that go beyond what would occur with a transactional approach alone. Moreover, transformational leadership is more than charisma. The purely charismatic leader may want followers to adopt the charismatic world view and go no further. The transformational leader will attempt to instill in followers the ability to question not only established views but also eventually those established by the leader.

Burns conceived leaders to be either transformational or transactional, but the paradigm was modified by **Bass** (1985–1985), who proposed that transformational leadership augments the effects of transactional leadership on the efforts, satisfaction, and effectiveness of subordinates. The transformational-transactional differentiation has formed the basis of sundry and other books since Burns's seminal work (Bass, 1985; Bennis & Nanus, 1985; Tichy & Devanna, 1986). Burns identified two types of political leadership transactional and transformational. The more traditional transactional leadership involves an exchange relationship between leaders and followers, but transformational leadership is based more on leaders shifting the values, beliefs and needs of their followers. An example of the later was the interviews with top executives of major companies conducted by Tichy and Devanna. They found that effective transformational leaders share the following characteristics–they identify themselves as change agents. They are courageous, they believe in people, they are value-driven, they are life long learners, they have the ability to deal with complexity, ambiguity and uncertainty, and they are visionaries.

The characteristics and approaches of transactional and transformational leaders based on research findings of **Bass** (1990).

Transactional Leaders

Contingent Reward: Contracts exchange of rewards for effort, promises rewards for good performance, recognizes accomplishments.

Management by Exception (active): Watches and searches for deviations from rules and standards, takes corrective action.

Management by Exception (passive): Intervenes only if standards are not met.

Laissez-faire: Abdicates responsibilities, avoids making decisions.

Transformational Leaders

Charisma: Provides vision and sense of mission, instills pride, gains respect and trust.

Inspiration: Communicates high expectations, uses symbols to focus efforts, expresses important purposes in simple ways.

Intellectual Stimulation: Promotes intelligence, rationality, and careful problem solving.

Individualized Consideration: Gives personal attention, treats each employee individually, coaches and advises.

Transformational leadership brings about change, innovation and entrepreneurship. They describe the process of corporate transformation that recognize the need for revitalization, created a new vision and institutionalize change (**Seltzer & Bass,** 1990).

According to Bass in many instances (such as relying on passive management by exception), transactional leadership is a prescription for mediocrity and that transformational leadership leads to superior performance in organizations facing demands for renewal and change. He suggests that fostering transformational leadership through policies of recruitment, selection, promotion, training and development will pay off in the health, well-being and effective performance of today's organizations.

Transformational leadership style emphasizes the importance of vision building and the ability to communicate this vision, and simultaneously, enthuse subordinates to make their vision a reality: 'to innovate, to change, and indeed to conquer new frontiers in the market place or on the shop floor (**Guest,** 1990).

Transformational leaders integrate creative insight, persistence and energy, intuition and sensitivity to the needs of others to forge the strategy-culture alloy for their organizations (**Bass, Avolio, & Bruce,** 1993).

Research has consistently demonstrated the superiority of transformational over transactional form of leadership, especially in the context of the present day turbulent organizational environment. (**E.g. Dubinsky,** *et al.*, 1995, **Yammarino, Spangler Bass,** 1993). Thus, hypothesizing that a leader with more of transformational leader style will have higher level of emotional intelligence. Subsequently, five sub hypothesis where formulated:

Transformational leaders adopt a long-term perspective rather than focusing solely on future needs; being concerned only with short-term problems and opportunities facing the organization, rather than viewing intra and extra organizational factors as discrete, they view them from a holistic orientation (**Dubinsky, Yammarino, Jolson, Spangler,** 1995).

Although transactional leadership can be positive force in an organization, transformational leadership is viewed as moving beyond this style and is characterized by motivating for performance beyond expectations, inspiring for missions beyond self-interest, and instilling confidence to achieve superior performance (**Carlson & Perrewe,** 1995).

Transformational leaders build confidence in followers, encouraging them to reframe the future and question the tried and true, and coaching them to develop their full capabilities (**Avolio, Howell & Sosik,** 1999).

Shamir and **Howell** (1999) proposed transformational organization impose fewer constraints on members activities, and offer fewer cues as to the appropriate behaviours, appeal to shared values and identities and linking members self-concepts to the organizational members to exercise discretion and suppress the expression of individual differences by both leaders and followers. Effective leadership entails the factors and dominions of vision trust, listening, authenticity, integrity, hope, addressing the true needs of the followers.

Research on transformational leadership (**Bass,** 1985, 1990, **Trichy and Devanna,** 1986, **Teppar,** 1993, **Keller,** 1992, **Chatterjee,** 1997, **Zohar,** 2001) has identified several characteristics of leadership. These become relevant to the degree to which organizations are transformational or transactional. Transactional leadership is reported (**Bass,** 1990) to be a prescription for mediocrity and transformational leadership is supposed to lead to superior performance in organizations facing demands for renewal and change.

Till date, effective leadership eludes many people and organizations, more so because, no quantitative research has been able to demonstrate which precise leadership behaviour would yield most positive result. Most of the leadership experts proffer advice based on inference, experience and instinct, which only at times is correct. Different scholars have attempted to categorize the leadership styles, but in practice, never any leader can be singled as adopting just one of the style. Thus, optimizing the mix of the different style to attain the highest level of effectiveness for a leader has been the main contention among the researchers (**Goleman** 2000). Here the research work of relevance (**Goleman,** 2000) suggested that it is the power and emotions that can help to decide upon the right style at right time and in the right measure.

Chapter 3

METHODOLOGY—INDIAN EXPERIENCES

FRAMEWORK OF THE STUDY

The present study is predominantly descriptive and diagnostic in nature. It has been intellectually exciting and rewarding, since the study offered opportunities to understand leadership dynamics from very close quarters.

It is an exploratory investigation undertaken to explore and compare the transactional functions and transformational dimensions, constituting corporate leadership and its relationship with role-efficacy in product and service organizations belonging to private, public and government sectors. The purpose was to examine the leadership effectiveness as a whole and the priorities assigned to transformational and transactional leadership functions by senior managers in relation to the role-efficacy in various select Indian organizations. The basic thesis behind this choice is that there is most probably a significant commonality in the profile of corporate leaders regardless of sectors they operate in.

The data for the study was obtained through five, leading, service and product based organizations in India. One was engaged in product manufacturing, belonging to private sector, other one was also product manufacturing, belonging to public sector, one was both product and service organization, belonging to private sector and two of them were service rendering, government of India organizations.

The selection of these organizations was based on specific purpose that organizations were identified as corporate leaders, to workout a relationship between corporate leadership and actualization of roles. The criterion of such assumption was based on corporate image and ownership, profits and development activities as per records in terms of financial allocation, physical target and achievement of short and long-term goals of the organizations.

DESIGN OF THE STUDY

The data for the study was obtained through five, leading, service and product based organizations in India. For the study of leadership at the senior level, many options and alternative approaches were followed. This is so because chief executives do not operate essentially within a limited and well-defined boundary Therefore, documentation through one approach would fail to offer a holistic picture. One way was through behaviour observation (functions). Yet another approach was by conducting survey using structured instruments and by personal interviews also. The study was designed to be conducted in three phases:

The first session comprised of administration of the questionnaire to the managers while they were on the job and collection of filled in questionnaires and personal meeting programmes with the subjects. To determine the functional factors contributing to effective leadership, it was felt appropriate to address the questionnaire to managerial cadre alone. Total 250 questionnaires were distributed in five different organizations. Out of 250, 208 questionnaires were received from the senior managers.

The questionnaire has two parts—first part deals with role-efficacy scale and second part deals with senior managers function schedule. Respondents were requested to go through the instructions given on the questionnaire and put their queries before filling out, during the survey. The respondents were assured that this was an academic exercise and their responses would be kept confidential and will be used for research purpose only. This assurance was further stated in the questionnaire. The questionnaire set was collected from the subjects, after few days or immediately as per completion of the sets as there was no time limit for completing the tests.

In the second phase, the subjects gave their reactions about the relevance of the items in the tools with their day-to-day functions and difficulties in filling in the questionnaires etc.

The third phase comprised of action phase. In this session the results of the responses to the questionnaire were correlated and discussed to arrive at conclusions and suggestions.

Sample

Incidental sampling method was used in selection of the subject's (senior managers) for the study. The study has covered 208 senior managers as respondents; composed of a comparatively small group of executives, *i.e.*, top and the middle management and is responsible for the overall management of the organization by establishing operating policies and practices, and thereby governing organization and its interaction with the environment. Efforts were made to take proportionate number of subjects working in five various services and products organizations belonging to public, private and government sectors. Table 3.1 reports, organization No.1 had a sample of 48 senior managers, organization No. 2 had a sample of 40 senior managers, organization No.3 had a sample of 50 senior managers, organization No. 4 had a sample of 35 senior managers and organization No. 5 had also a sample of 35 senior managers.

Table 3.1 Distribution of Respondents among Five Selected Organizations

Distribution of Respondents	*Organization No. 1*	*Organization No. 2*	*Organization No. 3*	*Organization No. 4*	*Organization No. 5*
Total Sample 208 (n = 208)	48 (n = 48)	40 (n = 40)	50 (n = 50)	35 (n = 35)	35 (n = 35)

Numerical Scoring System for Education of the Subjects

The subjects had various educational and technical qualifications. To bring a common numerical value to their qualifications for interpretational purposes, numerical system has been evolved, as follows:

Qualification (Educational / Technical) of Respondents	*Scores Awarded*
The subjects who studied upto X	10
The subjects who studied upto XII	12
The subjects who had completed diploma in engineering	13
The subjects who had completed graduation either B.Sc., B.A or B.Com	15
The subjects having bachelor degree in engineering like B.E. or B.Tech. or M.B.B.S.	16
The subjects who had completed post graduation either M.Sc., M.A or M.Com	17
The subjects having master degree like M.B.A , M.Tech or M.D	18
The subjects who had done Ph.D	19

Numerical Scoring for Diagnostics of Deficiency Percentages on Various Dimensions of Role-efficacy

In order to make a detailed Micro -level diagnostics of the deficiencies in various dimensions of role-efficacy and to develop interventions for enhancing role-efficacy, respondents were classified into five categories. Table below gives degrees of deficiencies alongwith percentages.

Categories	*Classification of Respondents According to Score in the Dimension of Role Efficacy*	*Percentages of Deficiencies in the Dimension*
1.	Who scored + 4.00	0% deficiencies
2.	Who scored + 3.00	25% deficiencies
3.	Who scored + 2.00	50% deficiencies
4.	Who scored + 1.00	75% deficiencies
5.	Who scored 0.00 & < 1	100% deficiencies

Numerical Scoring for Gender of the Participants

The numerical scoring system was developed for distinguishing the gender of the senior managers. It was 1 for Male and 2 for Female.

Numerical Scoring for Management Levels of the Respondents

The numerical scoring system was evolved for presenting the managerial cadre of the senior managers. It was 1 for Top management level and 2 for Middle management level.

Table 3.2 Demographic Variables (Age, Education, Experience, Gender And Management Level) of the Respondents with Mean Values and Scores of Standard Deviations of Organization No. 1.

S. No.	Variables	Mean	S.D
1.	Age	42.35	5.49
2.	Education	16.65	1.10
3.	Experience	19.63	6.63
4.	Gender	1.02	0.14
5.	Management Level	1.44	0.50

Table 3.3 Demographic Variables (Age, Education, Experience, Gender and Management Level) of the Respondents with Mean Values and Scores of Standard Deviations of Organization No. 2.

S. No.	Variables	Mean	S.D
1.	Age	38.18	4.73
2.	Education	16.78	1.49
3.	Experience	15.70	5.41
4.	Gender	1.10	0.30
5.	Management Level	1.25	0.44

Table 3.4 Demographic Variables (Age, Education, Experience, Gender and Management Level) of the Respondents with Mean Values and Scores of Standard Deviations of Organization No. 3.

S. No.	Variables	Mean	S.D
1.	Age	42.50	7.68
2.	Education	17.00	1.01
3.	Experience	17.68	9.53
4.	Gender	1.22	0.42
5.	Management Level	1.56	0.50

Table 3.5 Demographic Variables (Age, Education, Experience, Gender and Management Level) of The Respondents with Mean Values and Scores of Standard Deviations of Organization No. 4.

S. No.	Variables	Mean	S.D
1.	Age	42.80	3.93
2.	Education	16.54	1.48
3.	Experience	16.69	4.74
4.	Gender	1.03	0.17
5.	Management Level	1.34	0.48

Table 3.6 Demographic Variables (Age, Education, Experience, Gender and Management Level) of The Respondents with Mean Values and Scores of Standard Deviations of Organization No. 5.

S. No.	*Variables*	*Mean*	*S.D*
1.	Age	52.14	5.57
2.	Education	16.14	0.85
3.	Experience	28.29	6.47
4.	Gender	1.00	0.00
5.	Management Level	1.06	0.24

Means and SDs Scoring for Age of the Respondents

The standard practice was followed for rounding-off of age of the respondents. From Table 3.4 to 3.8, it would be seen that respondents ranged in the range of 30 yrs to 53 yrs with a Mean value of 42.35 and SD of 5.49 in organization 1, 29 yrs to 49 yrs with a Mean value of 38.18 and SD of 4.73 in organization 2, 30 yrs to 57 yrs with a Mean value of 42.50 and SD of 7.68 in organization 3, 30 yrs to 51 yrs with a Mean value of 42.80 and SD of 3.93 in organization 4 and 38 yrs to 58 yrs with a Mean value of 52.14 and SD of 5.57 in organization 5.

Means and SDs Scoring for Education of the Subjects

The standard practice was done for rounding-off of education of the subjects. Table 3.4 to 3.8, reports that subjects scored Mean of 16.65 and SD of 1.10 on education variable in organization 1, Mean of 16.78 and SD of 1.49 in organization 2, Mean of 17.00 and SD of 1.01 in organization 3, Mean value of 16.54 and SD of 1.48 in organization 4 and Mean of 16.14 and SD of 0.85 in organization 5.

Means and SDs Scoring for Experience of the Subjects

The rounding-off of experience of the senior managers was done following the standard practice. Table 3.4 to 3.8, presents that respondents ranged in experience between 7 yrs to 35 yrs with a Mean score of 19.63 and SD of 6.63 in organization 1, between 5 yrs to 27 yrs with a Mean score of 15.70 and SD of 5.41 in organization 2, between 2 yrs to 33 yrs with a Mean score of 17.68 and SD of 9.53 in organization 3, between 6 yrs to 28 yrs with a Mean score of 16.69 and SD of 4.74 in organization 4 and between 9 yrs to 35 yrs with a Mean score of 28.29 and SD of 6.47 in organization 5.

Means and SDs Scoring for Gender of the Participants

The rounding-off of gender difference was carried out following the standard practice. Table 3.4 to 3.8, depicts that participants scored Mean value of 1.02 and SD of 0.14 on gender variable in organization 1, Mean of 1.10 and SD of 0.30 in organization 2, Mean of 1.22 and SD of 0.42 in organization 3, Mean value of 1.03 and SD of 0.17 in organization 4 and Mean of 1.00 and SD of 0.00 in organization 5.

Means and SDs Scoring for Management Levels of Participants

The standard practice was followed for rounding-off of management level of the participants. Table 3.2 to 3.6, shows that respondents scored Mean of 1.44 and SD of 0.50 on management level in organization 1, Mean of 1.25 and SD of 0.44 in organization 2, Mean value of 1.56 and SD of 0.50 in organization 3, Mean of 1.34 and SD of 0.48 in organization 4 and Mean of 1.06 and SD of 0.24 in organization 5.

Tools/Instruments Used

For the purpose of data collection an extensive structured questionnaire of role-efficacy, developed by Pareek was used to diagnose the role-efficacy of the senior managers. To measure Corporate Leadership also, the method enumerated by Pareek was used. We chose this method as this measures the two relevant leadership styles transactional and transformational separately and simultaneously. The questionnaire pattern is given in appendix.

Role-Efficacy Scale

Role-Efficacy Scale (RES) has ten dimensions namely,

1. Centrality
2. Integration
3. Reactivity
4. Creativity
5. Inter role linkage
6. Helping relations
7. Super ordinations
8. Growth
9. Influence
10. Confrontation

The Instrument and its Administration

The role efficacy scale (RES) is a structured instrument consisting of twenty triads of statements. A respondent marks the one statement in each triad that describes his role most accurately. A role occupant for his role must complete the regular scale.

The three alternatives are pre-weighted. There are two statements for each dimension of role-efficacy and the scoring pattern followed is +2, +1 or-1.

Scoring

The scoring key is used for scoring responses as shown in appendix. Role efficacy index (REI) ranges from 0 to 100.

Reliability

Sen (1982) reported a retest reliability of .68 significant at .001 levels. This shows the high stability of the scale. Sen has also reported high internal consistency, indicated by significant correlation values among the items.

Validity

Sayeed (1985) reported item- total correlation for twenty RES items for a total sample of 658 managers, for eleven organizations separately. For the total sample the lowest correlation was 0.16 (for item 20) and the highest 0.51. The mean corrected item-total correlation for the entire sample was 0.36, with an alpha co-efficient of 0.80. The alpha co-efficients for the mean corrected item-total correlations of the eleven organizations ranged from 0.70 to 0.85. These results show internal homogeneity of the scale.

Senior Managerial Functions Schedule

Senior Managerial Function Schedule (SMFS) developed by **Udai Pareek** was used for the study. SMFS consists of a list of fourteen functions (seven are transactional and seven are transformational) as follows:

1. Policy making
2. Visioning
3. Planning
4. Modeling/inspiring
5. Setting standards
6. Developing systems
7. Monitoring performance
8. Boundary management
9. Coordinating
10. Synergising
11. Rewarding
12. Developing talent/mentoring
13. Coaching
14. Building culture and climate

The Instrument and its Administration

Senior Management Functions Schedule is designed to find out which transactional and transformational functions are being given priority by senior managers in an organization. The instrument is meant for the top leaders/senior managers.

SMFS consists of a list of fourteen functions (seven are transactional and seven are transformational). The respondent is required to indicate the priority of his attention/time to different functions by distributing hundred points among the fourteen listed functions.

Scoring

Scores given to each function gauge the priority of the function. The responses of senior managers are added to give a profile of the group. The various functions can also be rated on a scale from 1 to 10, although forced distribution of hundred points gives a more authentic profile. The total of transactional functions (items number 1, 3, 6, 7, 9, 11 and 13) and transformational functions (2, 4, 5, 8, 10, 12 and 14) may also be calculated.

Reliability

Cronbach Alpha for a group of 19 was found to be 0.94.

Validity

Responses from a group of eighteen senior insurance managers were factor analyzed (principal components analysis with varimax rotation). Factor analysis produced six factors, explaining eighty-five percent variance. The factor analysis provides construct validity of the instrument.

Factors 1, 3 and 5 contain seven transformational functions. These factors have been named HRD- institution building function, norm building function, synergising and boundary management function respectively. Three transactional factors are 2, 4 and 6. They are, respectively, policy-system development, promoting excellence and coordinating.

Techniques Used

Keeping in view the objectives of study, suitable statistical techniques were used for analysis of the data, as following:

Means and standard deviation were calculated in respect of each group of respondents in different organizations with regard to each of the 10 dimensions of the role-efficacy, 14 dimensions of the corporate leadership and demographic variables (age, education, experience, gender and management level).

The percentages of the deficiency of subjects with respect to each of the 10 dimensions of the role-efficacy were calculated.

For determining the relationship between various dimensions of role-efficacy and dimensions of the corporate leadership, inter-correlations were calculated.

Chapter 4

ANALYSIS AND RESULTS

The data collected through various tools and techniques was analyzed in reference to objectives of the study. Suitable statistical techniques were used for results and treatment of the data on need basis. From the descriptive statistics based on Means, Standard deviation and Intercorrelation in regard to 10 dimensions of Role efficacy, 14 components of Corporate Leadership Functions (Transactional and Transformational Dimensions) and Demographic Variables for 208 senior managers serving in 5 different organizations belonging to public, private and government sectors, analysis and interpretation of the data has been carried out.

High mean score suggests maximum number of responses of the subjects with regard to the respective dimension and vice-versa for low mean scores. On the other hand, High standard deviation value is indicative of the fact that there is a greater variation in the feelings and responses of the respondents with regard to the respective dimension. This suggests that some of the subjects might be having high scores while others might be having low scores on the concerned dimension. Low standard deviation thereby indicates similarity in the opinion of the participants with regard to the dimension.

MACRO-ANALYSIS

Role-Actualization Profiles of Organizations

To analyze Role-Efficacy Profile of participants, Means and SDs of scores on each of the 10 dimensions were calculated and are presented in the tables.

Mean Analysis

Table 4.1 depicts an overall picture of the responses of 48 senior managers in regard to various components of Role-Efficacy. It can be noticed that the respondents secured highest mean score on the dimension of Confrontation (Mean = 3.75). The second dimension on which the respondents' secured highest mean score was Inter-role linkage (Mean = 3.42). The III highest rank was observed for Integration (Mean = 3.38) and the mean scores for Helping relationship

(Mean = 3.21) was at the fourth highest position. Lowest rank was accorded by this group to Superordination (Mean=1.90), IX (II lowest) rank was accorded to Centrality (Mean=2.46), VIII (III lowest) rank was accorded to Proactivity (Mean = 2.58). VII rank, VI rank and V rank were accorded by this group to Influence (Mean=2.83), Creativity (Mean= 2.85) and Growth (Mean=2.88) respectively. The Means for Role-Efficacy Total (R.E.T) and Role-Efficacy Index (R.E.I) were 29.25 and 82.05 respectively. Based on the analysis presented above.

The Dominant dimensions for this group of participants were—Confrontation, Inter-role linkage, Integration and Helping relationship.

The Dormant dimensions for the select group of participants were—Superordination, Centrality and Proactivity.

The Backup dimensions for the select group of participants were—Growth, Creativity and Influence.

Table 4.1 Analysis of Role Efficacy Profile of Senior Managers of Organization No.1

S. No.	*Dimensions*	*Mean*	*Rank*	*SD*	*Rank*
1.	Centrality	2.46	9nth	0.74	10nth
2.	Integration	3.38	3rd	0.98	8rth
3.	Proactivity	2.58	8rth	1.30	3rd
4.	Creativity	2.85	6th	1.17	4rth
5.	Inter-role linkage	3.42	2nd	1.01	5th
6.	Helping relationship	3.21	4rth	1.46	2nd
7.	Superordination	1.90	10nth	1.52	1st
8.	Influence	2.83	7nth	1.00	6th
9.	Growth	2.88	5th	1.00	6th
10.	Confrontation	3.75	1st	0.79	9nth
11.	Role-efficacy total	29.25		6.32	
12.	Role-efficacy index	82.05		10.53	

(n = 48)

Standard Deviation Analysis

Looking into figures of SDs of various dimensions of Role-Efficacy as shown by the observed rank orders, by the respondents. It would be seen that highest SD was found for Superordination (SD = 1.52), the II highest rank was found for the component of Helping relationship (SD = 1.46), III highest rank was accorded to the dimension of Proactivity (SD = 1.30), and IV highest rank to Creativity (SD = 1.17). It is interesting to note that lowest SD was found in respect of Centrality (SD = 0.74), IX (II lowest) rank was observed for Confrontation (SD = 0.79) and VIII (III lowest) rank was accorded to Integration (SD = 0.98). The component of Inter-role linkage (SD = 1.01) was placed at V rank. Interestingly VI rank was accorded to Growth (SD = 1.00) and Influence (SD = 1.00) both. The Standard Deviations for Role-Efficacy Total (R.E.T) and Role-Efficacy Index (R.E.I) were 6.32 and 10.53 respectively. Hence,

The highest variability dimensions for the select group of participants were—Superordination, Helping relationship, Proactivity and Creativity.

The lowest variability dimensions for the select group of participants were—Centrality, Confrontation and Integration.

The moderate variability dimensions for the select group of participants were—Inter-role linkage, Growth and Influence.

Table 4.2 Analysis of Role Efficacy Profile of Senior Managers of Organization No. 2

S. No.	*Dimensions*	*Mean*	*Rank*	*SD*	*Rank*
1.	Centrality	2.58	7nth	0.98	8rth
2.	Integration	3.10	4rth	1.19	5th
3.	Proactivity	1.70	10nth	1.40	2nd
4.	Creativity	2.78	6th	1.21	4rth
5.	Inter-role linkage	328	3rd	1.13	7nth
6.	Helping relationship	3.50	1st	0.96	9nth
7.	Superordination	1.95	9nth	1.55	1st
8.	Influence	2.48	8rth	1.28	3rd
9.	Growth	2.85	5th	0.92	10nth
10.	Confrontation	3.35	2nd	1.14	6th
11.	Role-efficacy total	27.60		5.99	
12.	Role-efficacy index	79.30		10.00	

(n = 40)

Mean Analysis

Table 4.2 presents an overall picture of the feelings of 40 senior managers on various dimensions of Role-Efficacy as shown by the observed rank orders, by the respondents. It would be seen that this group had accorded highest rank to the Helping relationship (Mean= 3.50), the II highest rank to the component of Confrontation (Mean = 3.35), III highest rank to the dimension of Inter-role linkage (Mean = 3.28), and IV highest rank to Integration (Mean = 3.10). Lowest rank (X) was accorded by this group to Proactivity (Mean = 1.70), IX (II lowest) rank was assigned by this group to Superordination (Mean = 1.95), and VIII (III lowest) rank was accorded to Influence (Mean = 2.48). V rank was accorded to Growth (Mean = 2.85). The components of Creativity (Mean = 2.78) and Centrality (Mean = 2.58) were placed at VI and VII ranks respectively. The Mean values for Role-Efficacy Total and Role-Efficacy Index were 27.60 and 79.30 respectively. Hence,

The Dominant dimensions for the select group of participants were—Helping relationship, Confrontation, Inter-role linkage and Integration.

The Dormant dimensions for the select group of participants were—Proactivity, Superordination and Influence.

The Backup dimensions for the select group of participants were—Growth, Creativity and Centrality.

Standard Deviation Analysis

Looking into figures of SDs of various dimensions of Role-Efficacy as shown by the observed rank orders. It is interesting to not that highest rank order has been observed for the component of Superordination (SD = 1.55). The II highest rank has been assigned to the component of Proactivity (SD = 1.40) by the respondents. The III highest rank was found for Influence (SD = 1.28) and IV highest rank was for Creativity (SD = 1.21). Lowest rank was accorded by this group to Growth (SD = 0.92), IX (II lowest) rank was observed for Helping relationship (SD = 0.96), and VIII (III lowest) rank was accorded to Centrality (SD = 0.98). VII rank, VI rank and V rank were accorded by this group to Inter-role linkage (SD = 1.31), Confrontation (SD = 1.14) and Integration (SD = 1.19) respectively. The SDs for Role-Efficacy Total and Role-Efficacy Index were found 5.99 and 10.00 respectively.

Hence, the highest variability dimensions for the select group of participants were—Superordination, Proactivity, Influence and Creativity.

The lowest variability dimensions for the select group of participants were—Growth, Helping relationship and Centrality.

The moderate variability dimensions for the select group of participants were—Integration, Confrontation and Inter-role linkage.

Table 4.3 Analysis of Role Efficacy Profile of Senior Managers of Organization No. 3

S. No.	*Dimensions*	*Mean*	*Rank*	*SD*	*Rank*
1.	Centrality	2.16	7nth	1.56	5th
2.	Integration	2.78	3rd	1.23	10nth
3.	Proactivity	1.94	8rth	1.57	4rth
4.	Creativity	2.58	5th	1.44	7nth
5.	Inter-role linkage	2.66	4rth	1.53	6th
6.	Helping relationship	3.16	2nd	1.36	8rth
7.	Superordination	1.44	10nth	1.96	2nd
8.	Influence	1.76	9nth	2.01	1st
9.	Growth	2.20	6th	1.68	3rd
10.	Confrontation	3.20	1st	1.28	9nth
11.	Role-Efficacy Total	23.88		9.98	
12.	Role-Efficacy Index	73.10		16.63	

(n = 50)

Mean Analysis

Table 4.3 gives an overall picture of the responses 50 senior managers on various dimensions of Role-Efficacy. It can be seen that participants scored highest mean on the dimension of Confrontation (Mean = 3.20), followed by second highest mean on the dimension of Helping relationship (Mean = 3.16). The third highest mean was found on the dimension of Integration

(Mean = 2.78). Another point can be noticed from the table that the mean of IV highest rank was accorded to Inter-role linkage (Mean = 2.66) came approximately near to the mean of Integration. The Creativity (Mean = 2.58), Growth (Mean = 2.20) and Centrality (Mean = 2.16) were accorded V, VI and VII ranks respectively. Looking from the other side, it can be noticed that lowest mean was found on the dimension of Superordination (Mean = 1.44). The second lowest mean *i.e.*, higher than the lowest mean was found on the dimension of Influence (Mean = 1.76). The third lowest mean *i.e.*, higher than the second lowest mean was found on Proactivity (Mean = 1.94). The Means for Role-Efficacy Total and Role-Efficacy Index were 23.88 and 73.10 respectively. Hence,

The Dominant dimensions for the select group of participants were—Confrontation, Helping relationship, and Integration and Inter-role linkage.

The Dormant dimensions for the select group of participants were—Superordination, Influence and Proactivity.

The Backup dimensions for the select group of participants were—Creativity, Growth and Centrality.

Standard Deviation Analysis

Looking into figures of SDs for various dimensions of Role-Efficacy the highest rank order was found for Influence (SD = 2.01) the II highest rank was accorded to Superordination (SD = 1.96). The III highest rank was observed for Growth (SD = 1.68) and IV rank was assigned for Proactivity (SD = 1.57). Lowest rank was accorded by this group to Integration (SD = 1.23), IX (II lowest) rank has been observed for Confrontation (SD = 1.28), and VIII (III lowest) rank was accorded to Helping relationship (SD = 1.36). VII rank, VI rank and V rank were accorded by this group to Creativity (SD = 1.44), Inter-role linkage (SD = 1.53) and Centrality (SD = 1.56) respectively. The observed SDs for Role-Efficacy Total and Role-Efficacy Index were 9.98 and 16.63 respectively. Hence,

The highest variability dimensions for the select group of participants were—Influence, Superordination, Growth and Proactivity.

The lowest variability dimensions for the select group of participants were—Integration, Confrontation and Helping relationship.

The moderate variability dimensions for the select group of participants were—Centrality, Inter-role linkage and Creativity.

Mean Analysis

Table 4.4 depicts an overall picture of the feelings of 35 senior managers in regard to various components of Role-Efficacy. It is interesting to note that highest rank order has been assigned by the respondents to the component of Inter-role linkage (Mean = 3.26) the II highest rank was accorded to Helping relationship (Mean = 3.23) by the respondents. The III highest rank was for Confrontation (Mean = 3.20) and IV highest rank was assigned for Integration (Mean = 3.11). Lowest rank was accorded by this group to Superordination (Mean = 1.34), IX (II lowest) rank was accorded by this group to Proactivity (Mean = 1.94), and VIII (III lowest) rank was accorded to Creativity (Mean = 2.26). VII rank, VI rank and V rank were accorded by this group to Centrality

Table 4.4 Analysis of Role Efficacy Profile of Senior Managers of Organization No. 4

S. No.	Dimensions	Mean	Rank	SD	Rank
1.	Centrality	2.49	7nth	1.04	9nth
2.	Integration	3.11	4rth	1.25	8rth
3.	Proactivity	1.94	9nth	1.30	7nth
4.	Creativity	2.26	8rth	1.74	1st
5.	Inter-role linkage	3.26	1st	1.40	4rth
6.	Helping relationship	3.23	2nd	1.33	6th
7.	Superordination	1.34	10nth	1.64	2nd
8.	Influence	2.69	6th	1.35	5th
9.	Growth	2.80	5th	0.99	10nth
10.	Confrontation	3.20	3rd	1.59	3rd
11.	Role-efficacy total	26.31		7.51	
12.	Role-efficacy index	77.16		12.50	

(n = 35)

(Mean = 2.49), Influence (Mean = 2.69) and Growth (Mean = 2.80) respectively. The Means for Role-Efficacy Total and Role-Efficacy Index were 26.31 and 77.16 respectively. Hence,

The Dominant dimensions for the select group of participants were—Inter-role-linkage, Helping relationship, Confrontation and integration.

The Dormant dimensions for the select group of participants were—Superordination, Proactivity and creativity.

The Backup dimensions for the select group of participants were—Growth, Influence and centrality.

Standard Deviation Analysis

Looking into figures of SDs of various dimensions of Role-Efficacy ,it was seen that this group has accorded highest rank to the Creativity (SD = 1.74), the II highest rank was observed for the component of Super ordination (SD = 1.64), III highest rank was accorded to the dimension of Confrontation (SD = 1.59) and IV highest rank was accorded to Inter-role linkage (SD = 1.40). The Influence (SD = 1.35), Helping relations (SD = 1.33) and Proactivity (SD = 1.30) were accorded V, VI and VII ranks respectively. Lowest rank was found for Growth (SD = 0.99), II lowest rank was assigned to Centrality (SD = 1.04), and VIII (III lowest) rank was accorded to Integration (SD = 1.25). The Standard Deviations for Role-Efficacy Total and Role-Efficacy Index were found 7.51 and 12.50 respectively. Hence,

The highest variability dimensions for the select group of participants were—Creativity, Superordination, Confrontation and Inter-role linkage.

The lowest variability dimensions for the select group of participants were—Growth, Centrality and Integration.

The moderate variability dimensions for the select group of participants were—Influence, Helping relationship and Proactivity.

Table 4.5 Analysis of Role Efficacy Profile of Senior Managers of Organization No. 5

S. No.	*Dimensions*	*Mean*	*Rank*	*SD*	*Rank*
1.	Centrality	2.26	7nth	0.95	10nth
2.	Integration	2.63	5th	1.44	5th
3.	Proactivity	2.00	9nth	1.50	2nd
4.	Creativity	2.54	6th	1.22	8rth
5.	Inter-role linkage	3.17	3rd	1.38	6th
6.	Helping relationship	3.51	1st	0.98	9nth
7.	Superordination	1.89	10nth	1.62	1st
8.	Influence	2.74	4rth	1.27	7nth
9.	Growth	2.23	8rth	1.48	3rd
10.	Confrontation	3.34	2nd	1.47	4rth
11.	Role efficacy total	26.60		8.41	
12.	Role efficacy index	77.15		13.75	

(n = 35)

Mean Analysis

Table 4.5 presents the picture of the feeling of 35 senior managers on various dimensions of Role-Efficacy. It can be noticed that this group of senior managers had accorded the highest rank to the Helping relationship (Mean = 3.51). The II and III highest rank were accorded by the respondents to the component of Confrontation (Mean = 3.34) and Inter-role linkage (Mean = 3.17) respectively. IV highest rank was accorded to the dimension of Influence (Mean = 2.74) by this group. The component of Integration (Mean = 2.63), Creativity (Mean = 2.54), and Centrality (Mean = 2.26) were placed at V, VI and VII ranks respectively. Lowest rank was accorded to Superordination (Mean = 1.89), II lowest rank was assigned to Proactivity (Mean = 2.00), and III lowest (VIII) rank was accorded to Growth (Mean = 2.23). The Mean values for Role-Efficacy Total and Role-Efficacy Index were 26.60 and 77.15 respectively. Hence,

The Dominant dimensions for the select group of participants were—Helping relationship, Confrontation, Inter-role linkage and Influence.

The Dormant dimensions for the select group of participants were—Superordination, Proactivity and Growth.

The Backup dimensions for the select group of participants were—Integration, Creativity and Centrality.

Standard Deviation Analysis

Looking into figures of SDs of various dimensions of Role-Efficacy and their rank orders it would be seen that this group has assigned highest rank to the Superordination (SD = 1.62), the II highest rank was found for the component of Proactivity (SD = 1.50), III highest rank was accorded to the dimension of Growth (SD = 1.48), and IV highest rank to Confrontation (SD = 1.47). Lowest rank order (X) was observed for Centrality (SD = 0.95), IX (II lowest) rank was assigned by this group to Helping relations (SD = 0.98), and VIII (III lowest) rank was accorded to Creativity (SD = 1.22). V rank was found for Integration (SD = 1.44). The components of Inter-role linkage (SD = 1.38) and Influence (SD = 1.27) were placed at VI and VII ranks respectively. The SDs for Role-Efficacy Total and Role-Efficacy Index were 8.41 and 13.75 respectively. Hence,

The highest variability dimensions for the select group of participants were—Superordination, Proactivity, Growth and Confrontation.

The lowest variability dimensions for the select group of participants were—Centrality, Helping relationship and Creativity.

The moderate variability dimensions for the select group of participants were—Integration, Inter-role linkage and Influence.

Macro-analysis of Corporate Leadership Profile

In order to project an empirical picture of the profile of Transactional and Transformational Functions of senior managers of the organizations, Means and SDs on 14 functions were calculated and are presented in the tables.

Table 4.6 Profile Analysis of Corporate Leadership in Regard to Various Transactional Functions of Senior Managers of Organization No. 1

S. No.	*Functions*	*Mean*	*Rank*	*SD*	*Rank*
1.	Policy making	7.63	5th	3.77	3rd
2.	Planning	9.90	1st	4.79	2nd
3.	Developing systems	8.96	2nd	5.90	1st
4.	Monitoring performance	7.94	3rd	3.37	4rth
5.	Coordinating	7.75	4rth	3.13	5th
6.	Rewarding	6.40	6th	2.57	6th
7.	Coaching	6.04	7nth	2.19	7nth
	Average Mean	7.80			

(n = 48)

Profile Analysis of Corporate Leadership in Regard to Various Transactional Functions of Senior Managers of Organization No. 1

Table 4.6 depicts an overall picture of the priorities of 48 senior managers in regard to various components of Transactional Leadership functions. Rank orders have also been shown in the table. It is interesting to note that highest rank order has been assigned by the respondents to the component of Planning (Mean = 9.90). The II highest rank has been assigned to the component of Developing systems (Mean = 8.96) by the respondents. The III highest rank was for Monitoring performance (Mean = 7.94), the IV rank was for Coordination (Mean = 7.75). Lowest rank order was observed for Coaching (Mean = 6.04), II lowest rank was assigned by this group to Rewarding (Mean = 6.40), and III lowest rank was accorded to Policy making (Mean = 7.63). The Mean score was found to be 54.62 and Average Mean score for Transactional leadership functions was 7.80.Hence,

The Dominant dimensions for the select group of participants were—Planning, Developing systems and Monitoring performance.

The Dormant dimensions for the select group of participants were—Coaching, Rewarding and Policymaking.

The Backup dimension for the select group of participants was—Coordinating.

Variations in Regard to Various Dimensions of Transactional Leadership Functions of Senior Managers of Organization No. 1

Table 4.6 presents an overall picture of the feelings of 48 senior managers based on SDs of various dimensions of Transactional Leadership functions as shown by the observed rank orders, by the respondents. It would be seen that this group had accorded highest rank to the Developing systems (SD = 5.90), the II highest rank was found for the component of Planning (SD = 4.79), III highest rank was accorded to the dimension of Policy making (SD = 3.77). The component of Monitoring performance (SD = 3.37) was placed at IV rank. Interestingly this group accorded lowest rank to Coaching (SD = 2.19), II lowest rank was observed for Rewarding (SD = 2.57) and III lowest rank was accorded to Coordinating (SD = 3.13). Hence,

The highest variability dimensions for the select group of participants were—Developing systems, Planning and Policy making.

The lowest variability dimensions for the select group of participants were—Coaching, Rewarding and Coordinating.

The moderate variability dimension for the select group of participants was—Monitoring performance.

Table 4.7 Profile Analysis of Corporate Leadership in Regard to Various Transformational Functions of Senior Managers of Organization No. 1

S. No.	*Functions*	*Mean*	*Rank*	*SD*	*Rank*
1.	Visioning	7.23	2nd	2.50	3rd
2.	Modelling	6.52	3rd	3.41	1st
3.	Setting standards	6.50	4rth	2.40	5th
4.	Boundary management	5.54	7nth	2.07	7nth
5.	Synergising	5.73	6th	2.42	4rth
6.	Developing talent	6.46	5th	2.20	6th
7.	Building culture and climate	7.42	1st	3.29	2nd
	Average Mean	6.48			

(n = 48)

Profile Analysis of Corporate Leadership in Regard to Various Transformational Functions of Senior Managers of Organization No.1

Table 4.7 presents an overall picture of the responses of 48 senior managers in regard to various dimensions of Transformational Leadership functions. It can be noticed that highest importance has been assigned by the respondents to the component of Building culture and climate (Mean = 7.42). It is interesting to note that the II highest rank has been accorded to

Visioning (Mean = 7.23), which was followed by Modelling/Inspiring (Mean = 6.52). Lowest rank was accorded by this group to Boundary management (Mean = 5.54) II lowest rank to Synergising (Mean = 5.73) and III lowest rank to Developing talent/mentoring (Mean = 6.46). The component of Setting standards (Mean = 6.50) was placed at IV rank. The Total Mean value and Average Mean score for Transformational leadership functions were 45.4 and 6.48 respectively. Hence,

The Dominant dimensions for the select group of participants were—Building culture and climate, Visioning and Modelling.

The Dormant dimensions for the select group of participants were—Boundary management, Synergising and Developing talent.

The Backup dimension for the select group of participants was—Setting standards.

Variations in Regard to Various Dimensions of Transformational Leadership Functions of Senior Managers of Organization No. 1

From the Table 4.7 it would be further clear that highest variation among various functions was found in regard to Modelling (SD = 3.41) followed by Building culture and climate (SD = 3.29) and Visioning (SD = 2.50). It would be seen that these professionals had accorded lowest value to Boundary management (SD = 2.07), II lowest rank was observed for Developing talent (SD = 2.20) and III lowest rank was accorded to Setting standards (SD = 2.40). The dimension of Synergising (SD = 2.42) was placed at IV rank. Hence,

The highest variability dimensions for the select group of participants were—Modelling, Building culture and climate and Visioning.

The lowest variability dimensions for the select group of participants were—Boundary management, Developing talent and Setting standards.

The moderate variability dimension for the select group of participants was—Synergising.

Table 4.8 Profile Analysis of Corporate Leadership in Regard to Various Transactional Functions of Senior Managers of Organization No. 2

S. No.	*Functions*	*Mean*	*Rank*	*SD*	*Rank*
1.	Policy making	9.48	2nd	2.77	2nd
2.	Planning	10.40	1st	3.77	1st
3.	Developing systems	6.93	4rth	2.23	5th
4.	Monitoring performance	7.10	3rd	1.82	7nth
5.	Coordinating	6.30	6th	2.47	4rth
6.	Rewarding	6.40	5th	2.18	6th
7.	Coaching	6.13	7nth	2.49	3rd
	Average Mean	7.53			

(n = 40)

Profile Analysis of Corporate Leadership in Regard to Various Transactional Functions of Senior Managers of Organization No. 2

Table 4.8 presents an overall picture of the feelings of 40 senior managers on various dimensions of Transactional Leadership functions as shown by the observed rank orders, by the respondents. It would be seen that this group had accorded highest rank to the Planning (Mean= 10.40), the II highest rank was accorded by the respondents to the component of Policy making (Mean = 9.48), III highest rank was accorded to the dimension of Monitoring performance (Mean = 7.10). IV rank was assigned to Developing systems (Mean = 6.93). It is interesting to note that this group accorded lowest rank to Coaching (Mean = 6.13), this group assigned II lowest rank to Coordinating (Mean = 6.30), and III lowest rank was accorded to Rewarding (Mean = 6.40). The Total Mean value and Average Mean value for Transactional Leadership were 52.74 and 7.53 respectively. Hence,

The Dominant dimensions for the select group of participants were—Planning, Policy making and Monitoring performance.

The Dormant dimensions for the select group of participants were—Coaching, Coordinating and Rewarding.

The Backup dimension for the select group of participants was—Developing systems.

Variations in Regard to Various Dimensions of Transactional Leadership Functions of Senior Managers of Organization No. 2

Table 4.8 depicts an overall picture of the responses of 40 senior managers based on SDs of various dimensions of Transactional Leadership functions as shown by the observed rank orders. It is interesting to not that highest rank order has been observed for the component of Planning (SD = 3.77). The II highest rank has been assigned to the component of Policy making (SD = 2.77) by the respondents. The III highest rank was found for Coaching (SD = 2.49) and IV rank was observed for Coordinating (SD = 2.47). This group accorded lowest rank to Monitoring performance (SD = 1.82), II lowest rank was observed for Rewarding (SD = 2.18) and III lowest rank was accorded to Developing systems (SD = 2.23). Hence,

The highest variability dimensions for the select group of participants were—Planning, Policy making and Coaching.

The lowest variability dimensions for the select group of participants were—Monitoring performance, Rewarding and Developing systems.

The moderate variability dimension for the select group of participants was—Coordinating.

Table 4.9 Profile Analysis of Corporate Leadership in Regard to Various Transformational Functions of Senior Managers of Organization No.2

S. No.	Functions	Mean	Rank	SD	Rank
1.	Visioning	8.63	1st	2.89	2nd
2.	Modelling	6.53	4rth	2.25	4rth
3.	Setting standards	7.78	2nd	2.38	3rd
4.	Boundary management	5.55	6th	2.10	5th

5.	Synergising	5.25	7nth	2.03	7nth
6.	Developing talent	5.73	5th	2.09	6th
7.	Building culture and climate	7.73	3rd	4.23	1st
	Average Mean	6.74			

(n = 40)

Profile Analysis of Corporate Leadership in Regard to Various Transformational Functions of Senior Managers of Organization No. 2

It is interesting to note that Table 4.9 further depicts an overall picture of the feeling of 40 senior managers in regard to various components of Transformational Leadership functions. With respect to the responses of the managers, it can be noted that highest value had been given to Visioning (Mean = 8.63), followed by Setting standards (Mean = 7.78) and Building culture and climate (Mean = 7.73). The descriptive findings obtained here show that lowest rank was accorded by this group to Synergising (Mean = 5.25), II lowest rank was assigned by this group to Boundary management (Mean = 5.55) and III lowest rank was accorded to Developing talent (Mean = 5.73). It was observed that IV rank was assigned to Modelling (Mean = 6.53). Total Mean value and Average Mean value for Transformational Leadership were 47.2 and 6.74 respectively. Hence,

The Dominant dimensions for the select group of participants were—Visioning, Setting standards and Building culture and climate.

The Dormant dimensions for the select group of participants were—Synergising, Boundary management and Developing talent.

The Backup dimension for the select group of participants was—Modelling.

Variations in Regard to Various Dimensions of Transformational Leadership Functions of Senior Managers of Organization No. 2

Standard deviations of 40 senior managers on various dimensions of Transformational Leadership functions are also depicted in the Table 4.9. From the analysis it is further evident that, highest rank order has been accorded to the component of Building culture and climate (SD = 4.23). The II highest rank has been assigned to the component of Visioning (SD = 2.89) by the respondents. The III highest rank was observed for Setting standards (SD = 2.38) and IV rank was for Modelling (SD = 2.25). It is interesting to note that this group accorded lowest rank to Synergising (SD = 2.03), II lowest rank was observed for Developing talent (SD = 2.09) and III lowest rank was observed for Boundary management (SD = 2.10). Hence,

The highest variability dimensions for the select group of participants were—Building culture and climate, Visioning and Setting standards.

The lowest variability dimensions for the select group of participants were—Synergising, Developing talent and Boundary management.

The moderate variability dimension for the select group of participants was—Modelling.

Table 4.10 Profile Analysis of Corporate Leadership in Regard to Various Transactional Functions of Senior Managers of Organization No. 3

S. No.	Functions	Mean	Rank	SD	Rank
1.	Policy making	8.32	2nd	2.71	2nd
2.	Planning	9.00	1st	2.86	1st
3.	Developing systems	6.84	6th	2.17	4rth
4.	Monitoring performance.	7.44	3rd	2.32	3rd
5.	Coordinating.	7.16	4rth	1.66	7nth
6.	Rewarding.	6.86	5th	1.73	6th
7.	Coaching	6.08	7nth	2.06	5th
	Average Mean	7.38			

(n = 50)

Profile Analysis of Corporate Leadership in Regard to Various Transactional Functions of Senior Managers of Organization No. 3

Table 4.10 gives an overall picture of the responses 50 senior managers on various dimensions of Transactional Leadership functions. The interesting finding is that this group of senior managers had accorded the highest rank to the Planning (Mean=9.00), the II highest rank was accorded by the respondents to the component of Policy making (Mean=8.32, III highest rank was accorded to the dimension of Monitoring performance (Mean= 7.44) by this group and IV rank was accorded to Coordinating (Mean=7.16). The Coaching (Mean=6.08), Developing systems (Mean=6.84) and Rewarding (Mean=6.86) were accorded lowest, II lowest and III lowest ranks respectively. The Total Mean score and Average Mean score for Transactional Leadership were 51.7 and 7.38 respectively. Hence,

The Dominant dimensions for the select group of participants were—Planning, Policy making and Monitoring performance.

The Dormant dimensions for the select group of participants were—Coaching, Developing systems and Rewarding.

The Backup dimension for the select group of participants was—Coordinating.

Variations in Regard to Various Dimensions of Transactional Leadership Functions of Senior Managers of Organization No. 3

Table 4.10 reports rank orders between standard deviations scores in regard to various components of Transactional Leadership functions of 50 senior managers. It is interesting to note that the three high scoring dimensions turned out to be Planning (SD = 3.86) followed by Policy making (SD = 2.71) and Monitoring performance (SD = 2.32). IV rank was observed for Developing systems (SD = 2.17). Lowest score was noted for Coordinating (SD = 1.66), II lowest rank has been observed for Rewarding (SD = 1.73) and III lowest rank was observed for Coaching (SD = 2.06). Hence,

The highest variability dimensions for the select group of participants were—Planning, Policy making and Monitoring performance.

The lowest variability dimensions for the select group of participants were—Coordinating, Rewarding and Coaching.

The moderate variability dimension for the select group of participants was—Developing systems.

Table 4.11 Profile Analysis of Corporate Leadership in Regard to Various Transformational Functions of Senior Managers of Organization No. 3

S. No.	*Functions*	*Mean*	*Rank*	*SD*	*Rank*
1.	Visioning	8.48	1st	3.36	1st
2.	Modelling	6.48	5th	1.88	4rth
3.	Setting standards	7.88	2nd	2.20	2nd
4.	Boundary management	5.52	7nth	2.91	3rd
5.	Synergising	6.06	6th	1.68	7nth
6.	Developing talent	6.80	4rth	1.74	6th
7.	Building culture and climate	7.08	3rd	1.75	5th
	Average Mean	6.90			

(n = 50)

Profile Analysis of Corporate Leadership in Regard to Various Transformational Functions of Senior Managers of Organization No. 3

Table 4.11 further depicts an overall picture of the responses of 50 senior managers in regard to various dimensions of Transformational Leadership functions. It may be observed that this group of senior managers had also accorded the highest value to Visioning (Mean = 8.48), followed by Setting standards (Mean = 7.88) and Building culture and climate (Mean = 7.08). It would be further seen that lowest rank was accorded by this group to Boundary management (Mean = 5.52), II lowest rank was assigned by this group to Synergysing (Mean = 6.06) and III lowest rank was accorded to Modelling (Mean = 6.48). It was observed that IV rank was accorded to Developing talent (Mean = 6.80). The observed Total Mean value and Average Mean value for Transformational Leadership functions were 48.3 and 6.9 respectively. Hence,

The Dominant dimensions for the select group of participants were—Visioning, Setting standards and Building culture and climate.

The Dormant dimensions for the select group of participants were—Boundary management, Synergising and Modelling.

The Backup dimension for the select group of participants was—Developing talent.

Variations in Regard to Various Dimensions of Transformational Leadership Functions of Senior Managers of Organization No. 3

Table 4.11 further reports SDs of respondents on various functions of Transformational Leadership of 50 senior managers. It would be further seen that senior managers had accorded highest rank to Visioning (SD = 3.36), which was followed by Setting standards (SD = 2.20) and Boundary management (SD = 2.91). It is interesting to note that managers had assigned lowest score to Synergising (SD = 1.68) II lowest value was observed for Developing talent (SD = 1.74) and III lowest rank was accorded to Building culture and climate (SD = 1.75). The dimension of Modelling (SD = 1.88) was placed at IV rank. Hence,

The highest variability dimensions for the select group of participants were—Visioning, Setting standards and Boundary management.

The lowest variability dimensions for the select group of participants were—Synergising, Developing talent and Building culture and climate.

The moderate variability dimension for the select group of participants was—Modelling.

Table 4.12 Profile Analysis of Corporate Leadership in Regard to Various Transactional Functions of Senior Managers of Organization No. 4

S. No.	*Functions*	*Mean*	*Rank*	*SD*	*Rank*
1.	Policy making	11.48	2nd	6.64	1st
2.	Planning	11.97	1st	5.75	2nd
3.	Developing systems	6.94	3rd	3.54	5th
4.	Monitoring performance.	6.77	4rth	4.23	3rd
5.	Coordinating.	6.74	5th	4.02	4rth
6.	Rewarding.	5.80	6th	2.62	6th
7.	Coaching	5.51	7nth	2.50	7nth
	Average Mean	7.88			

(n = 35)

Profile Analysis of Corporate Leadership in Regard to Various Transactional Functions of Senior Managers of Organization No. 4

Table 4.12 presents rank orders between mean scores, of the responses of 35 senior managers in regard to various functions of Transactional Leadership. It is interesting to note that highest mean value has been assigned by the respondents to the component of Planning (Mean = 11.97) the II highest importance was accorded to Policy making (Mean = 11.48) by the respondents. The III highest rank score was for Developing systems (Mean = 6.94), whereas IV rank was assigned for the dimension of Monitoring performance (Mean = 6.77). Lowest rank was accorded by this group to Coaching (Mean = 5.51), II lowest rank was accorded by this group to Rewarding (Mean = 5.80) and III lowest rank was accorded to Coordinating (Mean = 6.74). The Total Mean value and Average Mean value for Transactional Leadership were 55.21 and 7.88 respectively. Hence,

The Dominant dimensions for the select group of participants were—Planning, Policy making and Developing systems.

The Dormant dimensions for the select group of participants were—Coaching, Rewarding and Coordinating.

The Backup dimension for the select group of participants was—Monitoring performance.

Variations in Regard to Various Dimensions of Transactional Leadership Functions of Senior Managers of Organization No. 4

Table 4.12 gives an overall picture of the responses 35 senior managers based on SDs of various dimensions of Transactional Leadership functions. It would be seen that this group had accorded highest rank to the Policy making (SD = 6.64), the II highest rank was observed for the component of Planning (SD = 5.75), III highest rank was accorded to the function of Monitoring performance (SD = 4.23) by this group and IV rank was observed for Coordinating (SD= 4.02). Lowest rank was found for Coaching (SD = 2.50), II lowest rank was assigned by this group to Rewarding (SD = 2.62) and III lowest rank was accorded to Developing systems (SD = 3.54). Hence,

The highest variability dimensions for the select group of participants were—Policy making, Planning and Monitoring performance.

The lowest variability dimensions for the select group of participants were—Coaching, Rewarding and Developing systems.

The moderate variability dimension for the select group of participants was— Coordinating.

Table 4.13 Profile Analysis of Corporate Leadership in Regard to Various Transformational Functions of Senior Managers of Organization No. 4

S.No.	Functions	Mean	Rank	SD	Rank
1.	Visioning	8.83	1st	6.05	1st
2.	Modeling	6.51	3rd	3.21	3rd
3.	Setting standards	5.80	6th	2.51	7nth
4.	Boundary management	4.94	7nth	2.93	5th
5.	Synergising	6.06	5th	3.14	4rth
6.	Developing talent	6.09	4rth	2.74	6th
7.	Building culture and climate	6.54	2nd	3.51	2nd
	Average Mean	6.39			

(*n* = 35)

Profile Analysis of Corporate Leadership in Regard to Various Transformational Functions of Senior Managers of Organization No.4

Table 4.13 further presents an overall picture of the responses of 35 senior managers in regard to various components of Transformational Leadership functions. It can be noticed that highest importance has been assigned by the respondents to the component of Visioning (Mean = 8.83), which was followed by Building culture and climate (Mean = 6.54) and Modelling/inspiring (Mean = 6.51). The component of Developing talent (Mean = 6.09) was placed at IV rank. The Boundary management (Mean = 4.94), Setting standards (Mean = 5.80) and Synergising (Mean = 6.06) were accorded lowest, II lowest and III lowest ranks respectively. The observed Total Mean value and Average Mean score for Transformational Leadership functions were 44.77 and 6.39 respectively. Hence,

The Dominant dimensions for the select group of participants were—Visioning, Building culture and climate and Modeling.

The Dormant dimensions for the select group of participants were—Boundary management, Setting standards and Synergising.

The Backup dimension for the select group of participants was—Developing talent.

Variations in Regard to Various Dimensions of Transformational Leadership Functions of Senior Managers of Organization No. 4

Standard deviations of 35 senior managers on various dimensions of Transformational leadership functions are depicted in the Table 4.13. From the analysis it may be further observed that, highest rank order has been accorded to the component of Visioning (SD = 6.05). The II highest rank has been assigned to the component of Building culture and climate (SD = 3.51) by the respondents. The III highest rank was observed for Modeling (SD = 3.21) and IV rank was observed for Synergising (SD = 3.14). It is interesting to note that this group accorded lowest rank to Setting standards (SD = 2.51), II lowest rank was observed for Developing talent (SD = 2.74) and III lowest rank was observed for Boundary management (SD = 2.93). Hence,

The highest variability dimensions for the select group of participants were—Visioning, Building culture and climate and Modelling.

The lowest variability dimensions for the select group of participants were—Setting standards, Developing talent and Boundary management.

The moderate variability dimension for the select group of participants was—Synergising.

Table 4.14 Profile Analysis of Corporate Leadership in Regard to Various Transactional Functions of Senior Managers of Organization No. 5

S.No.	*Functions*	*Mean*	*Rank*	*SD*	*Rank*
1.	Policy making	9.60	2nd	3.58	3rd
2.	Planning	10.51	1st	4.03	1st
3.	Developing systems	8.14	3rd	3.57	2nd
4.	Monitoring performance	7.34	5th	3.11	5th
5.	Coordinating	7.77	4rth	3.57	2nd
6.	Rewarding	5.34	7nth	1.94	7nth
7.	Coaching	6.00	6th	2.67	6th
	Average Mean	7.81			

(n = 35)

Profile Analysis of Corporate Leadership in Regard to Various Transactional Functions of Senior Managers of Organization No. 5

Table 4.14 presents the picture of the feeling of 35 senior managers on various dimensions of Transactional Leadership. It can be noticed that this group of senior managers had accorded the highest rank to the Planning (Mean = 10.51). The II and III highest rank were accorded by the respondents to the component of Policy making (Mean = 9.60) and Developing systems (Mean = 8.14) respectively. IV rank was accorded to the dimension of Coordinating (Mean = 7.77) by this group. Lowest rank was accorded to Rewarding (Mean = 5.34), II lowest rank was assigned to Coaching (Mean = 6.00) and III lowest rank was accorded to Monitoring performance (Mean = 7.34). The Total Mean value and Average Mean value for Transactional Leadership functions were found to be 54.7 and 7.81 respectively. Hence,

The Dominant dimensions for the select group of participants were—Planning, Policy making and Developing systems.

The Dormant dimensions for the select group of participants were—Rewarding, Coaching and Monitoring performance.

The Backup dimension for the select group of participants was—Coordinating.

Variations in Regard to Various Dimensions of Transactional Leadership Functions of Senior Managers of Organization No. 5

Table 4.14 presents an overall picture of the feelings of 35 senior managers based on SDs of various dimensions of Transactional Leadership as shown by the observed rank orders, by the respondents. It would be seen that this group has assigned highest value to the Planning (SD = 4.03), the II highest rank was found for the components of Developing systems and coordinating (SDs = 3.57) and III highest rank was accorded to the function of Policy making (SD = 3.58). Lowest mean score was observed for Rewarding (SD = 1.94), II lowest rank was assigned by this group to Coaching (SD = 2.67) and III lowest rank was observed for Monitoring performance (SD = 3.11). Hence,

The highest variability dimensions for the select group of participants were—Planning, Coordinating, Developing systems and Policy making.

The lowest variability dimensions for the select group of participants were—Rewarding, Coaching and Monitoring performance.

The moderate variability dimension for the select group of participants was—Monitoring performance.

Table 4.15 Profile Analysis of Corporate Leadership in Regard to Various Transformational Functions of Senior Managers of Organization No. 5

S.No.	*Functions*	*Mean*	*Rank*	*SD*	*Rank*
1.	Visioning	7.46	2nd	3.56	2nd
2.	Modeling	6.74	4rth	2.98	5th
3.	Setting standards	6.77	3rd	3.09	4rth
4.	Boundary management	5.11	6th	2.07	7nth
5.	Synergising	4.77	7nth	2.31	6th
6.	Developing talent	6.51	5th	3.35	3rd
7.	Building culture and climate	7.89	1st	7.82	1st
	Average Mean	6.46			

(n = 35)

Profile Analysis of Corporate Leadership in Regard to Various Transformational Functions of Senior Managers of Organization No. 5

Table 4.15 further depicts an overall picture of the responses of 35 senior managers in regard to various dimensions of Transformational Leadership functions. It is interesting to note that this group of senior managers had accorded the highest value to Building culture and climate (Mean = 7.89), followed by Visioning (Mean = 7.46) and Setting standards (Mean = 6.77). It would be further seen that lowest rank was accorded by this group to Synergising (Mean = 4.77), II lowest rank was assigned by this group to Boundary management (Mean= 5.11) and III lowest rank was accorded to Developing talent (Mean = 6.51). It was observed that IV rank was accorded to Modeling (Mean = 6.74). The observed Total Mean value and Average Mean value for Transformational Leadership functions were 45.25 and 6.46 respectively. Hence,

The Dominant dimensions for the select group of participants were—Building Culture and Climate, Visioning and Setting standards.

The Dormant dimensions for the select group of participants were—Synergising, Boundary management and Developing talent.

The Backup dimension for the select group of participants was—Modeling.

Variations in Regard to Various Dimensions of Transformational Leadership Functions of Senior Managers of Organization No. 5

Table 4.15 further presents an overall picture of the responses of 35 senior managers in regard to various components of Transformational Leadership functions based on observed rank orders of standard deviations. It can be noticed that highest rank order has been assigned by the respondents to the component of Building culture and climate (SD = 7.82), which was followed by Visioning (SD = 3.56) and Developing talent (SD = 3.35). The component of Setting standards (SD = 3.09) was placed at IV rank. The Boundary management (SD = 2.07), Synergising (SD = 2.31) and Modeling (SD = 2.98) were accorded lowest, II lowest and III lowest ranks respectively. Hence,

The highest variability dimensions for the select group of participants were—Building culture and climate, Visioning and Developing talent.

The lowest variability dimensions for the select group of participants were—Boundary management, Synergising and Modeling.

The moderate variability dimension for the select group of participants was—Setting standards.

Profile Analysis of Corporate Leadership Regarding Transactional Functions along all the Five Organizations

The dominant dimensions of corporate leadership along five different organizations were Planning, Policy making and Developing systems.

The dormant dimensions of corporate leadership along five different organizational settings were Coaching, Rewarding and Coordinating.

The backup dimensions of corporate leadership along five different organizations was Monitoring performance.

Profile Analysis of Corporate Leadership Regarding Transformational Functions along all the Five Organizations

The dominant dimensions of corporate leadership along five different organizations were Visioning, Building culture and climate and Setting standards.

The dormant dimensions of corporate leadership along five different organizational settings were Boundary management, Synergising and Developing talent.

The backup dimensions of corporate leadership along five different organizations was Modelling.

MICRO-ANALYSIS

Diagnostics of Deficiency Percentages in Various Dimensions of Role–Efficacy of Senior Managers among Different Organizations at Micro Level

As mentioned in the methodology the respondents who scored 4.00 on a dimension were supposed to have full efficiency *i.e.*, 100% efficacy in that dimension. It is to be recalled that 4 is the highest score one can obtain on any of the 10 dimensions of Role - Efficacy. The score 3 represents a deficiency of 25% while a score of 2 and 1 reflect deficiency of 50% and 75% respectively. Similarly, scores 0 and less are supposed to indicate a deficiency of 100%. The adequacy and inadequacy of role-incumbents is clearly indicated in the distribution of percentages obtained for Senior Managers serving in various organizations across 10 Role -Efficacy dimensions to draw inferences based on the preliminary qualitative analysis.

Deficiency Percentages in Various Dimensions of Role–Efficacy of Senior Managers in Organization No. 1

The four high scoring dimensions under Role-Efficacy Profile analysis were Confrontation, Inter-role linkage, Integration and Helping relationship. The low scores under Role-Efficacy audit were noted for Superordination, Centrality and Proactivity. The three backup dimensions were found to be Growth, Creativity and Influence. These findings gives a substantial support to the results reported in regard to Micro-analysis carried out for identifying percentages of respondents having deficiencies on various dimensions of Role-Efficacy.

From the Table 4.16 it can be seen that on Centrality dimension only 6/48% of the respondents had full efficacy in their role. On the other hand 42/48% of the respondents had deficiencies in this dimension in varying degrees. For example, 11/48% respondents had 25% deficiencies, 30/48% respondents had 50% deficiencies and 1/48% had 75% deficiencies. What was more striking that none had 100% deficiencies on this dimension?

Table 4.16 Deficiency Percentages in Various Dimensions of Role–Efficacy of Senior Managers of Organization No. 1

S.No.	*Dimensions*	*0% Score = (4)*	*25% Score = (3)*	*50% Score = (2)*	*75% Score = (1)*	*100% Score = (0 to -2)*
1.	Centrality	6/48	11/48	30/48	1/48	0/48
2.	Integration	29/48	12/48	5/48	0/48	2/48
3.	Proactivity	9/48	25/48	6/48	3/48	5/48
4.	Creativity	18/48	14/48	9/48	5/48	2/48
5.	Inter-role linkage	30/48	14/48	0/48	2/48	2/48

6.	Helping relationship	34/48	4/48	1/48	6/48	3/48
7.	Superordination	1/48	23/48	11/48	2/48	11/48
8.	Influence	13/48	19/48	13/48	1/48	2/48
9.	Growth	15/48	16/48	15/48	0/48	2/48
10.	Confrontation	43/48	1/48	1/48	3/48	0/48

(n = 48)

As regard to the third highest dimension of Integration, it can be seen that percentage of persons having no deficiency in regard to integrating their knowledge, skill and expertise to meet the demand of role, is approximately similar to the second highest dimension of Inter-role linkage, 29/48%. However, differences in regard to degrees of deficiencies can be noticed *i.e.,* 19/48%. However it is worth attention that 12/48% of the respondents had 25% deficiencies, 5/48% respondents had 50% deficiencies. It is also interesting to note that 0/48% had 75% deficiencies and the rest 2/48% had 100% deficiencies with respect to this dimension of Integration.

It can be seen that on the dimension of proactivity only 9/48% of the respondents had full efficacy in their role. On the other hand 39/48% of the respondents had deficiencies in this dimension in varying degrees. For example 25/48% respondents had 25% deficiencies, 6/48% respondents had 50% deficiencies, only 3/48% respondents had 75% deficiencies and 5/48% respondents had 100% deficiencies in their perception about their roles.

On the dimension of creativity, it is encouraging to note that 18/48% respondents had clear and correct perception of this dimension. On the other hand 30/48% of the respondents had deficiencies in this dimension in varying degrees. However it is worth noticing that 14/48% of the respondents had 25% deficiencies, 9/48% had deficiency upto the extent of 50%, 5/48% had deficiencies upto the extent of 75% and remaining 2/48% had deficiencies upto 100%.

It can be seen that on Inter-role linkage dimension, which is the second dominant dimension, here also the percentage of subjects having no deficiency was 30/48% which offer support to the results reported in respect of mean value. However, the percentage of participants having deficiency upto the level of 25% was quite large 14/48%, it gives further insight into the analysis of cases requiring help. On the other hand 18/48% of the respondents had deficiencies in this dimension in varying degrees. Interestingly, 0/48% respondents had 50% deficiencies, only 2/48% respondents had 75% deficiencies and 2/48% respondents had 100% deficiencies in their perception.

On the dimension of Helping relationship, which was also found to be dominant, it is significant to note that 34/48% of the respondents had no deficiency. However, on the other hand 14/48% of the respondent had deficiencies on this dimension from 25% to 100%. For example, 4/48% respondents had 25% deficiencies, it is more striking that only 1/48% respondents had 50% deficiencies, 6/48% respondents had 75% deficiencies and 3/48% respondents had 100% deficiencies in their perception.

Micro-analysis brings to light very significant information. It can be seen that on Superordination dimension only 1/48% of the respondents had full efficacy in their role. On the other hand, 47/48% of the respondents had deficiencies in this dimension in varying degrees. For example, 23/48% respondents had 25% deficiencies, 11/48% respondents had 50% deficiencies, it is worth attention that only 2/48% respondents had 75% deficiencies. Remaining, 11/48%, too large respondents had 100% deficiencies in their perception of roles.

In regard to Influence 13/48% had no deficiency. On the other hand, 35/48% of the respondents had deficiencies in this dimension in varying degrees. For example, 19/48% respondents had 25% deficiencies, 13/48% respondents had 50% deficiencies, it is worth attention that only 1/48% respondents had 75% deficiencies and 2/48% had 100% deficiency.

It can be seen that on Growth dimensions 15/48% of the respondents had full efficacy in their role. On the other hand, 33/48% of the respondents had deficiencies in this dimension in varying degrees. For example, 16/48% respondents had only marginal deficiency to the extent of 25%, 15/48% respondents had deficiency upto 50%, it is worth attention that 0/48% respondents had 75% deficiencies and remaining 2/48% respondents had difficulty upto 100% in their perception.

It can be observed from the Table 4.16 that percentage of participants having no deficiency on the dimension of Confrontation was found to be highest *i.e.*, 43/48%. This gives a substantial support to results reported in respect of observed mean score on the dimension of Confrontation. On the other hand, 5/48% of the respondents had deficiencies in this dimension in varying degrees. The percentage of respondents having deficiency to extent of 25% and 50% being equal i.e., 1/48% also substantiates the results. However, there were 3/48% respondents having deficiency upto the degree of 75%. It is interesting to note that none had 100% deficiencies in their perception.

Deficiency Percentages in Various Dimensions of Role–Efficacy of Senior Managers in Organization No. 2

On the whole, Helping relationship, Confrontation, Inter-role linkage and Integration components of Role-Efficacy were figured as high scoring dimensions under Role-Efficacy Profile analysis, whereas Proactivity, Superordination and Influence in that order emerged as low ranking dimensions, while, Growth, Creativity and Centrality showed backup Mean values. This data analysis substantiates the results observed in respect to Micro-level diagnostics of the deficiencies on various dimensions of Role-Efficacy.

Table 4.17 Deficiency Percentages in Various Dimensions of Role–Efficacy of Senior Managers in Organization No. 2

S.No.	*Dimensions*	*0% Score = (4)*	*25% Score = (3)*	*50% Score = (2)*	*75% Score = (1)*	*100% Score = (0 to -2)*
1.	Centrality	8/40	11/40	19/40	0/40	2/40
2.	Integration	21/40	8/40	8/40	0/40	3/40
3.	Proactivity	3/40	12/40	8/40	4/40	13/40
4.	Creativity	12/40	16/40	7/40	1/40	4/40
5.	Inter-role linkage	25/40	8/40	0/40	7/40	0/40
6.	Helping relationship	29/40	6/40	1/40	4/40	0/40
7.	Superordination	6/40	12/40	9/40	2/40	11/40
8.	Influence	5/40	22/40	6/40	3/40	4/40
9.	Growth	11/40	14/40	14/40	0/40	1/40
10.	Confrontation	28/40	5/40	0/40	7/40	0/40

(*n*=40)

Table 4.17 depicts that on Centrality dimension 8/40% of the respondents had full efficacy in their role. On the other hand, 32/40% of the respondents had deficiencies in this dimension in varying degrees. For example, 11/40% respondents had 25% deficiencies, 19/40% respondents had 50% deficiencies. What is more striking is none had 75% deficiencies on this dimension. It is interesting to note that only 2/40% had 100% deficiencies with respect to this dimension.

On the dimension of Integration it is encouraging to note that 21/40% respondents had clear perception of role integration *i.e.*, full efficacy in their role. On the other hand, 19/40% of the respondents had deficiencies in this dimension in varying degrees. However, it is worth attention that 8/40% of the respondents had 25% deficiencies, again 8/40% respondents had 50% deficiencies. It is also interesting to note that 0/40% had 75% deficiencies. The remaining 3/40% had 100% deficiencies in their perception regarding this component.

It is interesting to note that on the dimension of Proactivity only 3/40% of the respondents had full efficacy in their role. On the other hand, 37/40% of the respondents had deficiencies in this dimension in varying degrees. Like, 12/40% respondents had 25% deficiencies, 8/40% respondents had 50% deficiencies, only 4/40% respondents had 75% deficiencies and 13/40% respondents had 100% deficiencies with respect to this dimension.

On the dimension of Creativity it is encouraging to note that 12/40% respondents had clear and correct perception of this dimension *i.e.*, 100% efficacy in this dimension. On the other hand, 28/40% of the respondents had deficiencies in this dimension in varying degrees. It is worth attention that 16/40% of the respondents had 25% deficiencies, 7/40% respondents had 50% deficiencies, only 1/40% had 75% deficiencies and 4/40% had 100% deficiencies in their perception.

It can be seen that on the dimension of Inter-role linkage 25/40% of the respondents had full efficacy in their role. On the other, hand, 15/40% of the respondents had deficiencies in this dimension in varying degrees. For example, 8/40% respondents had 25% deficiencies, interestingly, 0/40% respondents had 50% deficiencies, 7/40% respondents had 75% deficiencies and it is worth attention that 0/40% respondents had 100% deficiencies in their perception.

On the dimension of Helping Relationship it is encouraging to note that 29/40% of the respondents had full efficacy on this dimension. On the other hand, 11/40% of the respondent had deficiencies in this dimension in varying degrees. For example, 6/40% respondents had 25% deficiencies, it is more striking that only 1/40% respondents had 50% deficiencies, 4/40% respondents had 75% deficiencies and no one had 100% deficiencies in their perception regarding this dimension.

It can be seen that on Superordination dimension only 6/40% of the respondents had full efficacy in their role. On the other hand, 34/40% of the respondents had deficiencies in this dimension in varying degrees. Like, 12/40% respondents had 25% deficiencies, 9/40% respondents had 50% deficiencies, only 2/40% respondents had 75% deficiencies and rest 11/40% respondents had 100% deficiencies on this dimension.

On the dimension of Influence only 5/40% of the respondents had full efficacy in their role. On the other hand, 35/40% of the respondents had deficiencies in this dimension in varying degrees. For example, 22/40% respondents had 25% deficiencies, 6/40% respondents had 50% deficiencies, it is worth attention that only 3/40% respondents had 75% deficiencies and 4/40% respondents had 100% deficiencies with respect to this dimension.

On the dimension of Growth 11/40% of the respondents had full efficacy. On the other hand, 29/40% of the respondents had deficiencies in this dimension in varying degrees. For example,

14/40% respondents had 25% deficiencies, again 14/40% respondents had 50% deficiencies, it is worth attention that 0/40% respondents had 75% deficiencies and just 1/40% respondent had 100% deficiencies in their perception.

On the dimension of Confrontation, it is very encouraging to note that 28/40% of respondents had clear perception *i.e.*, full efficacy. On the other hand, 12/40% of the respondents had deficiencies in this dimension in varying degrees. For example, only 5/40% respondent had 25% deficiencies and none had 50% deficiencies, 7/40% respondents had 75% deficiencies. It is striking to note that 0/40% respondents had 100% deficiencies on this dimension.

Table 4.18 Deficiency Percentages in Various Dimensions of Role–Efficacy of Senior Managers in Organization No. 3

S. No.	*Dimensions*	*0% Score = (4)*	*25% Score = (3)*	*50% Score = (2)*	*75% Score = (1)*	*100% Score = (0 to -2)*
1.	Centrality	10/50	11/50	20/50	1/50	8/50
2.	Integration	19/50	12/50	11/50	5/50	3/50
3.	Proactivity	8/50	16/50	7/50	5/50	14/50
4.	Creativity	16/50	12/50	15/50	3/50	4/50
5.	Inter-role linkage	21/50	12/50	3/50	9/50	5/50
6.	Helping relationship	32/50	8/50	0/50	6/50	4/50
7.	Superordination	6/50	16/50	5/50	4/50	19/50
8.	Influence	8/50	17/50	9/50	3/50	13/50
9.	Growth	12/50	14/50	12/50	2/50	10/50
10.	Confrontation	33/50	5/50	3/50	7/50	2/50

(n = 50)

Deficiency Percentages in Various Dimensions of Role–Efficacy of Senior Managers in Organization No. 3

Role-Efficacy audit reports high mean values for Confrontation, Helping relationship, and Integration and Inter-role linkage. The dimensions having poor ratings were Superordination, Influence and Proactivity. The three backup dimensions were found to be Creativity, Growth and Centrality under Role-Efficacy Profile analysis. These findings gives a substantial support to the results reported in respect to Micro-analysis carried out for identifying percentages of participants having deficiencies on various dimensions of Role-Efficacy.

Table 4.18 reports that on the dimension of Centrality 10/50% of the respondents had full efficacy in their role. On the other hand, 40/50% of the respondents had deficiencies in this dimension in varying degrees. Like for example, 11/50% respondents had 25% deficiencies, 20/50% respondents had 50% deficiencies, only 1/50% had 75% deficiencies and 8/50% had 100% deficiencies on this dimension.

On the dimension of Integration it is encouraging to note that 19/50% respondents had clear perception and had full efficacy on this dimension. On the other hand, 31/50% of the respondents had deficiencies in this dimension in varying degrees. However, it is to worth attention that 12/50% of the respondents had 25% deficiencies, 11/50% respondents had 50% deficiencies. It is also interesting to note that 5/50% had 75% deficiencies and 3/50% had 100% deficiencies with respect to this dimension of Integration.

It can be seen that on the dimension of Proactivity only 8/50% of the respondents had full efficacy in their role. On the other hand, 42/50% of the respondents had deficiencies in this dimension in varying degrees. For example, 16/50% respondents had 25% deficiencies, 7/50% respondents had 50% deficiencies, only 5/50% respondents had 75% deficiencies and 14/50% respondents had 100% deficiencies in their perception about their roles.

On the dimension of Creativity it is encouraging to note that 16/50% respondents had clear and correct perception *i.e.*, full efficacy on this dimension. On the other hand, 34/50% of the respondents had deficiencies in this dimension in varying degrees. It is interesting to note that 12/50% of the respondents had 25% deficiencies, 15/50% respondents had 50% deficiencies, 3/50% had 75% deficiencies and 4/50% had 100% deficiencies with respect to this dimension.

It can be seen that on Inter-role linkage dimension 21/50% of the respondents had full efficacy in their role. On the other hand, 29/50% of the respondents had deficiencies in this dimension in varying degrees. Like, 12/50% respondents had 25% deficiencies, interestingly, 3/50% respondents had 50% deficiencies, 9/50% respondents had 75% deficiencies and 5/50% respondents had 100% deficiencies in their perception.

On the dimension of Helping relationship it is encouraging to note that 32/50 of the respondents had clear and correct perception of this dimension. On the other hand, 18/50% of the respondent had deficiencies in this dimension in varying degrees. For example, 8/50% respondents had 25% deficiencies, it is more striking to note that 0/50% respondents had 50% deficiencies, 6/50% respondents had 75% deficiencies and 4/50% respondents had 100% deficiencies on this dimension.

It can be seen that on Superordination dimension only 6/50% of the respondents had full efficacy in their role. On the other hand, 44/50% of the respondents had deficiencies in this dimension in varying degrees. For example, 16/50% respondents had 25% deficiencies, 5/50% respondents had 50% deficiencies, it is worth attention that only 4/50% respondents had 75% deficiencies and 19/50% respondents had 100% deficiencies with respect to this dimension.

On the dimension of Influence 8/50% of the respondents had full efficacy in their role. On the other hand, 42/50% of the respondents had deficiencies in this dimension in varying degrees. For example, 17/50% respondents had 25% deficiencies, 9/50% respondents had 50% deficiencies, it is important to note that only 3/50% respondents had 75% deficiencies and 13/50% respondents had 100% deficiencies in their perception.

It can be seen that on Growth dimensions 12/50% of the respondents had full efficacy in their role. On the other hand, 38/50% of the respondents had deficiencies in this dimension in varying degrees. For example, 14/50% respondents had 25% deficiencies, 12/50% respondents had 50% deficiencies, it is worth noticing that only 2/50% respondents had 75% deficiencies and 10/50% respondents had 100% deficiencies on this dimension.

On the dimension of Confrontation, it is important to note that 33/50% of respondents had full efficacy. On the other hand, 17/50% of the respondents had deficiencies in this dimension in varying degrees. For example, 5/50% respondent had 25% deficiencies and 3/50% respondents had 50% deficiencies, and 7/50% respondents had 75% deficiencies. It is interesting to note that only 2/50% respondents had 100% deficiencies in their perception on this dimension.

Table 4.19 Deficiency Percentages in Various Dimensions of Role–Efficacy of Senior Managers in Organization No. 4

S. No.	*Dimensions*	*0% Score = (4)*	*25% Score = (3)*	*50% Score = (2)*	*75% Score = (1)*	*100% Score = (0 to -2)*
1.	Centrality	6/35	11/35	14/35	2/35	2/35
2.	Integration	19/35	5/35	10/35	0/35	1/35
3.	Proactivity	5/35	8/35	7/35	10/35	5/35
4.	Creativity	9/35	13/35	2/35	4/35	7/35
5.	Inter-role linkage	24/35	5/35	0/35	5/35	1/35
6.	Helping relationship	24/35	4/35	0/35	5/35	2/35
7.	Superordination	3/35	6/35	9/35	5/35	12/35
8.	Influence	8/35	18/35	5/35	0/35	4/35
9.	Growth	11/35	8/35	15/35	0/35	1/35
10.	Confrontation	27/35	0/35	1/35	4/35	3/35

(n = 35)

Deficiency Percentages in Various Dimensions of Role–Efficacy of Senior Managers in Organization No. 4

The results of the Role-Efficacy Profile analysis revealed dominant dimensions for the select group of participants were Inter-role linkage, Helping relationship, Confrontation and Integration where as the dormant dimensions were Superordination, Proactivity and Creativity and the backup dimensions for the select group of participants were Growth, Influence and Centrality, seems to be in line with Micro-analysis carried out for identifying percentages of subjects having deficiencies on various dimensions of Role-Efficacy.

Table 4.19 presents the further analysis that on Centrality dimension only 6/35% of the respondents had full efficacy in their role. On the other hand, 29/35% of the respondents had deficiencies in this dimension in varying degrees. For example, 11/35% respondents had 25% deficiencies, 14/35% respondents had 50% deficiencies and only 2/35% had 75% deficiencies and again only 2/35% had 100% deficiencies on this dimension.

On the dimension of Integration, it is encouraging to note that 19/35% respondents had clear perception of role integration. *i.e.* full efficacy in their role. On the other hand 16/35% of the respondents had deficiencies in this dimension in varying degrees. However it is worth attention that 5/35% of the respondents had 25% deficiencies, 10/35% respondents had 50% deficiencies. It is also interesting to note that 0/35% had 75% deficiencies and only 1/35% had 100% deficiencies with respect to this dimension of Integration.

It is interesting to note that on the dimension of Proactivity only 5/35% of the respondents had full efficacy in their role. On the other hand 30/35% of the respondents had deficiencies in this dimension in varying degrees. For example 8/35% respondents had 25% deficiencies, 7/35% respondents had 50% deficiencies, 10/35% respondents had 75% deficiencies and 5/35% respondents had 100% deficiencies in their perception about this dimension in their roles.

On the dimension of Creativity it is encouraging to note that only 9/35% respondents had clear and correct perception of this dimension. On the other hand, 26/35 % of the respondents had deficiencies in this dimension in varying degrees. However, it is worth attention that 13/35% of the respondents had 25% deficiencies, only 2/35% respondents had 50% deficiencies, 4/35% had 75% deficiencies and 7/35% had 100% deficiencies with respect to this dimension.

It can be seen that on Inter-role linkage dimension, 24/35% of the respondents had full efficacy in their role. On the other hand, 11/35% of the respondents had deficiencies in this dimension in varying degrees. For example, 5/35% respondents had 25% deficiencies, interestingly, 0/35% respondents had 50% deficiencies, 5/35% respondents had 75% deficiencies and only 1/35% respondents had 100% deficiencies in their perception on this dimension.

On the dimension of Helping relationship it is encouraging to note that 24/35% of the respondents had clear and correct perception of this dimension. On the other hand, 11/35% of the respondents had deficiencies in this dimension in varying degrees. For example, 4/35% respondents had 25% deficiencies, it is more striking that 0/35% respondents had 50% deficiencies, 5/35% respondents had 75% deficiencies and only 2/35% respondents had 100% deficiencies in their perception with respect to this dimension.

It can be seen that on Superordination dimension only 3/35% of the respondents had full efficacy in their role. On the other hand, 32/35% of the respondents had deficiencies in this dimension in varying degrees. For example, 6/35% respondents had 25% deficiencies, 9/35% respondents had 50% deficiencies, it is worth attention that only 5/35% respondents had 75% deficiencies and 12/35% respondents had 100% deficiencies in their perception of roles regarding this dimension.

On the dimension of Influence, interestingly only 8/35% of the respondents had full efficacy in their role. On the other hand, 27/35% of the respondents had deficiencies in this dimension in varying degrees. For example, 18/35% respondents had 25% deficiencies, 5/35% respondents had 50% deficiencies, it is worth attention that 0/35% respondents had 75% deficiencies and 4/35% respondents had 100% deficiencies in their perception.

It can be seen that on Growth dimensions 11/35% of the respondents had full efficacy in their role. On the other hand, 24/35% of the respondents had deficiencies in this dimension in varying degrees. For example, 8/35% respondents had 25% deficiencies, 15/35% respondents had 50% deficiencies, it is worth attention that 0/35% respondents had 75% deficiencies and only 1/35% respondents had 100% deficiencies in their perception.

On the dimension of Confrontation, it is very encouraging to note that 27/35% of respondents had clear and correct perception. On the other hand, only 8/35% of the respondents had deficiencies in this dimension in varying degrees. For example, it is interesting to note that none respondent had 25% deficiencies, only 1/35% respondents had 50% deficiencies, and 4/35% respondents had 75% deficiencies and 3/35% respondents had 100% deficiencies in their perception.

Table 4.20 Deficiency Percentages in Various Dimensions of Role–Efficacy of Senior Managers in Organization No. 5

S. No.	*Dimensions*	*0% Score = (4)*	*25% Score = (3)*	*50% Score = (2)*	*75% Score = (1)*	*100% Score = (0 to -2)*
1.	Centrality	3/35	9/35	20/35	0/35	3/35
2.	Integration	11/35	11/35	8/35	1/35	4/35
3.	Proactivity	6/35	11/35	4/35	5/35	9/35
4.	Creativity	8/35	12/35	10/35	1/35	4/35
5.	Inter-role linkage	21/35	8/35	0/35	5/35	1/35
6.	Helping relationship	26/35	5/35	0/35	4/35	0/35
7.	Superordination	5/35	9/35	11/35	1/35	9/35
8.	Influence	9/35	16/35	6/35	2/35	2/35
9.	Growth	7/35	8/35	13/35	4/35	3/35
10.	Confrontation	28/35	1/35	0/35	4/35	2/35

(n = 35)

Deficiency Percentages in Various Dimensions of Role-Efficacy of Senior Managers in Organization No. 5

A close examination of the observed findings of Role-Efficacy audit presents a strong degree of commonality between the results of Role-Efficacy Profile analysis and the deficiency values obtained by Micro -level diagnostics of the deficiencies on various dimensions of Role-Efficacy *i.e.,* the top scoring dimensions for the select group of participants were Helping relationship, Confrontation, Inter-role linkage and Influence. The low ranking dimensions were Superordination, Proactivity and Growth and the backup dimensions turned out to be Integration, Creativity and Centrality.

From Table 4.20 it would be observed that on Centrality dimension only 3/35% of the respondents had full efficacy in their role. On the other hand, 32/35% of the respondents had deficiencies in this dimension in varying degrees. For example, 9/35% respondents had 25% deficiencies, 20/35% respondents had 50% deficiencies and interestingly 0/35% had 75% deficiencies and only 3/35% had 100% deficiencies with regard to this dimension.

On the dimension of Integration it is encouraging to note that 11/35% respondents had full efficacy in their role. On the other hand, 24/35% of the respondents had deficiencies in this dimension in varying degrees. However, it is worth attention that 11/35% of the respondents had 25% deficiencies, 8/35% respondents had 50% deficiencies, only 1/35% had 75% deficiencies and 4/35% had 100% deficiencies on this dimension of Integration.

It is interesting to note that on the dimension of Proactivity only 6/35% of the respondents had full efficacy in their role. On the other hand, 29/35% of the respondents had deficiencies in this dimension in varying degrees. For example, 11/35% respondents had 25% deficiencies, 4/35% respondents had 50% deficiencies, 5/35% respondents had 75% deficiencies and 9/35% respondents had 100% deficiencies in their perception.

On the dimension of Creativity only 8/35% respondents had clear and correct perception of this dimension. On the other hand, 27/35% of the respondents had deficiencies in this dimension in varying degrees. However, it is worth attention that 12/35% of the respondents had 25% deficiencies, 10/35% respondents had 50% deficiencies, only 1/35% had 75% deficiencies and 4/35% had 100% deficiencies with respect to this dimension.

It can be seen that on Inter-role linkage dimension 21/35% of the respondents had full efficacy in their role. On the other hand, 14/35% of the respondents had deficiencies in this dimension in varying degrees. For example, 8/35% respondents had 25% deficiencies, interestingly, 0/35% respondents had 50% deficiencies, 5/35% respondents had 75% deficiencies and only 1/35% respondents had 100% deficiencies on this dimension.

On the dimension of Helping relationship it is encouraging to note that 26/35% of the respondents had clear and correct perception of this dimension. On the other hand, 9/35% of the respondent had deficiencies in this dimension in varying degrees. For example, 5/35% respondents had 25% deficiencies, it is more striking that 0/35% respondents had 50% deficiencies, 4/35% respondents had 75% deficiencies and again 0/35% respondents had 100% deficiencies in their perception with respect to this dimension.

It can be seen that on Superordination dimension only 5/35% of the respondents had full efficacy in their role. On the other hand, 30/35% of the respondents had deficiencies in this dimension in varying degrees. For example, 9/35% respondents had 25% deficiencies, 11/35% respondents had 50% deficiencies, it is worth attention that only 1/35% respondents had 75% deficiencies and 9/35% respondents had 100% deficiencies in their perception of roles regarding this dimension.

On the dimension of Influence, interestingly only 9/35% of the respondents had full efficacy in their role. On the other hand, 26/35% of the respondents had deficiencies in this dimension in varying degrees. For example, 16/35% respondents had 25% deficiencies, 6/35% respondents had 50% deficiencies, it is worth attention that 2/35% respondents had 75% deficiencies and 2/35% respondents had 100% deficiencies in their perception regarding this dimension.

It can be seen that on Growth dimensions 7/35% of the respondents had full efficacy in their role. On the other hand, 28/35% of the respondents had deficiencies in this dimension in varying degrees. For example, 8/35% respondents had 25% deficiencies, 13/35% respondents had 50% deficiencies, it is worth attention that 4/35% respondents had 75% deficiencies and only 3/35% respondents had 100% deficiencies in their perception.

On the dimension of Confrontation, it is interesting to note that 28/35% of respondents had full efficacy. On the other hand, 7/35% of the respondents had deficiencies in this dimension in varying degrees. For example, only 1/35% respondent had 25% deficiencies and strikingly none respondents had 50% deficiencies, 4/35% respondents had 75% deficiencies and only 2/35% respondents had 100% deficiencies in their perception on this dimension.

INTERCORRELATION ANALYSIS

*** Denotes that coefficient of correlation (r) is significant at 0.001 level of significance $p<0.001$

** Denotes that coefficient of correlation (r) is significant at 0.01 level of significance $p<0.01$

* Denotes that coefficient of correlation (*r*) is significant at 0.05 level of significance $p<0.05$
NS Denotes that $p>0.05$ meaning not significant.

Analysis of Intercorrelations Between Role-Efficacy and Corporate Leadership for Senior Managers

Table 4.21. Analysis of Corporate Leadership Components (Transactional Functions and Transformational Functions) as Related to Role-Efficacy Total for Senior Managers of Organization No. 1

Corporate Leadership Functions	*Role Efficacy Total*
Transactional components	
Policy making	0.09
Planning	0.19
Developing systems	–0.12
Monitoring performance	–0.18
Co-ordinating	–0.19
Rewarding	–0.06
Coaching	0.04
Transformational Components	
Visioning	0.16
Modelling	0.09
Setting standards	0.08
Boundary management	–0.07
Synergising	–0.03
Developing talent	–0.09
Building culture and climate	0.11

(n = 48)

Analysis of Corporate Leadership Components (Transactional Functions and Transformational Functions) as Related to Role-Efficacy Total for Senior Managers of Organization No. 1

Table 4.21 examines intercorrelational results among variables under consideration as follows:
Role efficacy total, positively related with Policymaking ($r = 0.09$)
Role efficacy total, positively related with Visioning ($r = 0.16$)
Role efficacy total, positively related with Planning ($r = 0.19$)
Role efficacy total, positively related with Modeling ($r = 0.09$)
Role efficacy total, positively related with Setting standards ($r = 0.08$)
Role efficacy total, negatively related with Developing systems ($r = -0.12$)

Role efficacy total, negatively related with Monitoring performance (*r* = – 0.18)
Role efficacy total, negatively related with Boundary management (*r* = – 0.07)
Role efficacy total, negatively related with Coordinating (*r* = – 0.19)
Role efficacy total, negatively related with Synergising (*r* = – 0.03)
Role efficacy total, negatively related with Rewarding (*r* = – 0.06)
Role efficacy total, negatively related with Developing talent (*r* = – 0.09)
Role efficacy total, positively related with Coaching (*r* = 0.04)
Role efficacy total, positively related with Building culture and climate (*r* = 0.11)

Table 4.22 Analyses of Corporate Leadership Components (Transactional Functions and Transformational Functions) as Related to Role-Efficacy Total for Senior Managers of Organization No. 2

Corporate Leadership Functions	*Role Efficacy Total*
Transactional Components	
Policy making	0.37*
Planning	– 0.03
Developing systems	– 0.06
Monitoring performance	– 0.12
Coordinating	– 0.34**
Rewarding	0.11
Coaching	0.08
Transformational Components	
Visioning	0.16
Modelling	– 0.33**
Setting standards	0.08
Boundary management	– 0.21
Synergising	– 0.07
Developing talent	– 0.14
Building culture and climate	0.20

(*n* = 40)

Analysis of Corporate Leadership Components (Transactional Functions and Transformational Functions) as Related to Role-Efficacy Total for Senior Managers of Organization 2.

Table 4.22 presents intercorrelational results among variables under consideration as follows:

Role efficacy total, positively related with Policymaking (*r* = 0.37)*
Role efficacy total, positively related with Visioning (*r* = 0.16)
Role efficacy total, negatively related with Planning (*r* = – 0.03)
Role efficacy total, negatively related with Modeling (*r* = – 0.33)**
Role efficacy total, positively related with Setting standards (*r* = 0.08)
Role efficacy total, negatively related with Developing systems (*r* = – 0.06)

Role efficacy total, negatively related with Monitoring performance ($r = -0.12$)
Role efficacy total, negatively related with Boundary management ($r = -0.21$)
Role efficacy total, negatively related with Coordinating ($r = -0.34$)**
Role efficacy total, negatively related with Synergising ($r = -0.07$)
Role efficacy total, positively related with Rewarding ($r = 0.11$)
Role efficacy total, negatively related with Developing talent ($r = -0.14$)
Role efficacy total, positively related with Coaching ($r = 0.08$)
Role efficacy total, positively related with Building culture and climate ($r = 0.20$)

Table 4.23 Analysis of Corporate Leadership Components (Transactional Functions and Transformational Functions) as Related to Role-Efficacy Total for Senior Managers of Organization No. 3

Corporate Leadership Functions	*Role Efficacy Total*
Transactional Components	
Policy making	−0.23
Planning	−0.16
Developing systems	0.08
Monitoring performance	0.04
Coordinating	−0.26
Rewarding	0.00
Coaching	−0.16
Transformational Components	
Visioning	0.09
Modelling	0.12
Setting standards	0.34*
Boundary management	0.01
Synergising	0.04
Developing talent	0.23
Building culture and climate	−0.11

($n = 50$)

Analysis of Corporate Leadership Components (Transactional Functions and Transformational Functions) as Related to Role-Efficacy Total for Senior Managers of Organization 3.

Table 4.23 depicts intercorrelational results among variables under consideration as follows:

Role efficacy total, negatively related with Policymaking ($r = -0.23$)
Role efficacy total, positively related with Visioning ($r = 0.09$)
Role efficacy total, negatively related with Planning ($r = -0.16$)
Role efficacy total, positively related with Modeling ($r = 0.12$)
Role efficacy total, positively related with Setting standards ($r = 0.34$)*

Role efficacy total, positively related with Developing systems ($r = 0.08$)

Role efficacy total, positively related with Monitoring performance ($r = 0.04$)

Role efficacy total, positively related with Boundary management ($r = 0.01$)

Role efficacy total, negatively related with Coordinating ($r = -0.26$)

Role efficacy total, positively related with Synergising ($r = 0.04$)

Role efficacy total, positively related with Rewarding ($r = 0.00$)

Role efficacy total, positively related with Developing talent ($r = 0.23$)

Role efficacy total, negatively related with Coaching ($r = -0.16$)

Role efficacy total, negatively related with Building culture and climate ($r = -0.11$)

Table 4.24 Analysis of Corporate Leadership Components (Transactional Functions and Transformational Functions) as Related to Role-Efficacy Total for Senior Managers of Organization No. 4

Corporate Leadership Functions	*Role Efficacy Total*
Transactional Components	
Policy making	0.15
Planning	0.41*
Developing systems	−0.17
Monitoring performance	−0.02
Coordinating	−0.07
Rewarding	−0.22
Coaching	−0.27
Transformational Components	
Visioning	0.19
Modelling	0.09
Setting standards	0.05
Boundary management	−0.21
Synergising	−0.45**
Developing talent	−0.08
Building culture and climate	−0.12

($n = 35$)

Analysis of Corporate Leadership Components (Transactional Functions and Transformational Functions) as Related to Role-Efficacy Total for Senior Managers of Organization 4.

Table 4.24 reports intercorrelational results among variables under consideration as follows:

Role efficacy total, positively related with Policymaking ($r = 0.15$)

Role efficacy total, positively related with Visioning ($r = 0.19$)

Role efficacy total, positively related with Planning ($r = 0.41$)*

Role efficacy total, positively related with Modeling ($r = 0.09$)

Role efficacy total, positively related with Setting standards ($r = 0.05$)

Role efficacy total, negatively related with Developing systems ($r = -0.17$)

Role efficacy total, negatively related with Monitoring performance ($r = -0.02$)

Role efficacy total, negatively related with Boundary management ($r = -0.21$)

Role efficacy total, negatively related with Coordinating ($r = -0.07$)

Role efficacy total, negatively related with Synergising ($r = -0.45$)**

Role efficacy total, negatively related with Rewarding ($r = -0.22$)

Role efficacy total, negatively related with Developing talent ($r = -0.08$)

Role efficacy total, negatively related with Coaching ($r = -0.27$)

Role efficacy total, negatively related with Building culture and climate ($r = -0.12$)

Table 4.25 Analysis of Corporate Leadership Components (Transactional Functions and Transformational Functions) as Related to Role-Efficacy Total for Senior Managers of Organization No. 5

Corporate Leadership Functions	*Role Efficacy Total*
Transactional Components	
Policy making	0.22
Planning	0.34*
Developing systems	0.23
Monitoring performance	– 0.05
Coordinating	0.01
Rewarding	– 0.31
Coaching	– 0.05
Transformational Components	
Visioning	0.21
Modelling	– 0.08
Setting standards	0.36*
Boundary management	0.22
Synergising	– 0.08
Developing talent	– 0.38*
Building culture and climate	– 0.35*

($n = 35$)

Analysis of Corporate Leadership Components (Transactional Functions and Transformational Functions) as Related to Role-Efficacy Total for Senior Managers of Organization 5.

Table 4.25 reports intercorrelational results among variables under consideration as follows:

Role efficacy total, positively related with Policymaking ($r = 0.22$)

Role efficacy total, positively related with Visioning ($r = 0.21$)

Role efficacy total, positively related with Planning ($r = 0.34$)*

Role efficacy total, negatively related with Modeling ($r = -0.08$)

Role efficacy total, positively related with Setting standards ($r = 0.36$)*

Role efficacy total, positively related with Developing systems ($r = 0.23$)

Role efficacy total, negatively related with Monitoring performance ($r = -0.05$)

Role efficacy total, positively related with Boundary management ($r = 0.22$)

Role efficacy total, positively related with Coordinating ($r = 0.01$)

Role efficacy total, negatively related with Synergising ($r = -0.08$)

Role efficacy total, negatively related with Rewarding ($r = -0.31$)

Role efficacy total, negatively related with Developing talent ($r = -0.38$)*

Role efficacy total, negatively related with Coaching ($r = -0.05$)

Role efficacy total, negatively related with Building culture and climate ($r = -0.35$)*

Chapter 5

CONCLUSIONS AND SUGGESTIONS

CONCLUSIONS

In view of the growing global competition in the market place, information and technology explosion, increasing complexities in the external and internal environment, total quality service revolution, globalization, liberalization of economy changing demographics, upheavals in societal values, high expectation level of the workforce etc, organizations will need to be flexible and will have to look out for finding out new strategies to survive and to become successful.

The study attempts to find out the relationship between Corporate Leadership and Role Efficacy of Senior Managers representing a wide variety of work environments unique in their characteristics. The intent of this research was to study functional profiles of senior managers by means of the roles they have to perform, affecting the organizational effectiveness. This research is based on study of managerial leadership from a sample of 208 Indian managers from 5 Indian organizations belonging to private and government sectors. The study emphatically distinguishes between transactional (management) and transformational (leadership) functions of corporate leadership in organizations and argues that quest for managerial leadership is essentially a transformational journey towards new identity.

Data was generated through questionnaire method and various phases of observation to yield qualitative and quantitative information, that has been statically treated and complemented by rank–orders, mean–analysis, standard deviations and correlation–analysis, in order to explore whether there is any relationship between corporate leadership and role-efficacy as well as the priorities assigned to transactional and transformational functions of corporate leadership, and also to identify deficient dimensions of role-efficacy among senior managers as a part of their managerial efficacy. To make a detailed micro-level diagnostics of the deficiencies in various dimensions of role-efficacy at the micro-level, respondents were classified into five categories on a continuum from extremely deficient to not at all deficient.

Though subjects have all the potentials and skills for going ahead and meeting the targets of organizations, provided the barriers coming in their way are removed through appropriate interventions by developing the corporate culture, as people in managerial positions complain repeatedly that they are held responsible for things over which they have little control.

It is exemplified by the fact that the Indian has more reverence for survival and security and because of this; it is difficult to find a spirit of survival with excellence. The absence of this spirit has led to an orientation to perpetuate and maintain the status quo, rather than making efforts to explore the possibilities of innovation and change. Personal attributes alone are insufficient for managers to lead until unless supported by the top management. In the present context, therefore, the management will have to play not only the role of a thinker but equally the role of a doer, meaning thereby getting closely associated with the implementation phase of change too.

Main Findings

The present study reveals a significant homogeneity in the profiles of senior managers in giving priority to Transactional functions (Average Mean Value, for Organization 1= 7.80, for Organization 2 =7.53, for Organization 3 = 7.38, for Organization 4 = 7.88, for Organization 5 = 7.81, respectively) over Transformational functions (Average Mean Value, for Organization 1 = 6.48, for Organization 2 = 6.74, for Organization 3 = 6.90, for Organization 4 = 6.39, for Organization 5 = 6.46 respectively) among all the five organizations (Table 12 to 21 in chapter 4).

The analysis brings into focus the deficient areas of Role-Efficacy namely Superordination, Centrality, Proactivity, Influence, Creativity and Growth, and dominant dimensions namely Confrontation, Inter-role linkage, Integration and Helping relationship (Table 7 to 11 and table 22 to 26 of chapter 4).

A thorough probe into the values of intercorrelations between 10 dimensions of role-efficacy and 14 components of corporate leadership functions indicates clearly that dimensions of the corporate leadership are related positively as well as negatively with role-efficacy total, upto various degrees and significance level (Table 27 to 31 of chapter 4).

Conclusion drawn from the foregoing analysis gives an impression and hint towards the existing state of affairs in the organization and posses a question about the organizational culture prevailing in the organizational built-up by the corporate policy makers, which perhaps may not be conducive to appreciate the new ideas of corporate transformation and as a consequence managers are compelled to give priority to the transactional leadership over transformational leadership in their operating leadership styles to survive and to maintain their existence in the organization.

SUGGESTIONS

The analysis of the data throws up some pertinent issues for managers. The responses of senior managers were analyzed and deficiency areas were identified to suggest action plans for corporate transformation. The issue here is one of specifying the possible stages of transition that an enterprise may have to go through towards becoming a corporate leader by devising policies, practices, and cultural norms to foster both transactional and transformational functions of corporate leadership in a conjoint manner.

There should be essentially dyadic pattern of relationships between top and other levels of management in a relatively flat structure with fewer hierarchical levels, low formalization, wide spans of control, by loosening the organizational structure, giving operational autonomy and extending support to managers at the micro and macro level to function more effectively.

Challenges Ahead

To craft the right mission.

To build a strong corporate image.

To ensure that top management is committed.

To provide a comprehensive global perspective for organization.

To develop a corporate culture that inspires every employee.

To ensure that each and every employee in the company is involved and important.

To realize that competitive advantage and core competence is must for survival.

To attain total quality in every sphere.

To cope with incessant global change.

To create an energized workforce that evolves with the organization.

To be an excellent organization by whatever criteria.

To be strategically alert and future-oriented.

To facilitate the achievement of productivity, quality and profits.

To adhere to ethical practices for building long-term competitive edge.

To fulfill the interests and needs of the customer through the products and services.

To match organizational objectives to individual aspirations.

To allow people to see the big picture.

To make individuals and company more flexible.

To create a learning organization.

To break down bureaucratic barriers to new ideas.

To establish performance plans for the company and individuals.

To ensure a transparent and open communication across functions and people.

To ensure that every employee is empowered and has the autonomy to plan and organize his or her work.

To evolve a responsive and participative style of management.

To mix business with pleasure.

To ensure that every employee in the company has a sense of pride and ownership in the quality of the work they do.

To ensure excellent working conditions, satisfied and motivated employees.

To become an organization which believes in pursuit of excellence alone.

To assure that your service to anyone must provide great advantage and equally great disadvantage if not provided.

Building Blocks of Leadership

In the past seventy years more than 3,000 leadership studies have been conducted and dozens of leadership models and theories have been proposed. Although we have access to an overwhelming volume of leadership theory and research, few guidelines exist which are of use to practitioners. Nevertheless, interest in leadership and in those qualities, which separate a successful leader from and unsuccessful one, remains unabated.

Successful corporate leaders in today's demanding environment tend to share certain personal characteristics. Although leadership research has not revealed a single trait that is possessed by all successful leaders, a number of characteristics have been identified that are common to many of them provided, freedom for action should be accepted as a basic premise for leadership .The future manager will be exceptionally skillful by the following to become a corporate leader:

Believes to serve as role models.

Believes in strong vision and planning.

Believes in integrity and consistency.

Believes in excellent communication and social skills.

Believes in positive mental attitude.

Believes in teamwork and empowerment.

Believes in effective resources management.

Believes in fact-based decision-making.

Believes in emotional stability.

Believes in adaptability and initiative taking.

Believes in courage and determination.

Believes in endurance and dynamism.

Believes in mastering and mentoring.

Believes in effective information management.

Believes in business knowledge and professional skills.

Believes in technical knowledge and conceptual skills.

Believes in creativity and core competence.

Believes in risk taking and flexibility.

Believes in sense of responsibility.

Believes in awareness of self and surroundings.

Believes in intelligence and intellectual energy.

Believes in drive and persistence.

Believes in analytical judgment and rationality.

Believes in good sense of humor.

Believes in achieving ambition with perseverance.

Believes in aggressiveness and assertiveness at times.

Believes in effective organizing and coordination.

Believes in democracy as well as diplomacy.

Believes in becoming structured and organized.

Believes in establishing high ethical standards.

Believes in individual and task orientations.

Believes in time and goal orientation.

Believes in self-confidence and enlightenment.

Believes in benchmarking and continuous learning.

Believes in caring and nurturing.

Believes in firmness on virtues and values.

Believes in winning with wits and wisdom.

Believes in entrepreneurship and charisma.

Believes in constant customer focus.

Believes in implementing different strategies for different situation.

Believes in effective knowledge management.

Believes in transforming with speed.

Believes in autonomy and decentralization.

Believes in openness and receptivity.

Believes in trust and transparency.

Believes in approachability and listening.

Believes in passion and becoming a change agent.

Believes in adequate manpower planning.

Believes in right recruitment and placement.

Believes in effective performance and potential appraisal.

Believes in career development and career planning.

Believes in continuous training and development.

Believes in effective feedback and counseling.

Believes in linking rewards with performance.

Believes in zeal and diligence.

Believes in challenging the status quo.

Believes in motivating and inspiring.

Believes in monitoring performance and funds.

Believes in consultative and participative approach.

Believes in directness and commitment.

Believes in conflict resolution skills.

Believes in multicultural skills.

Believes in credibility and objectivity.

Believes in dominance and extroversion.

Believes in warmth and empathy.

Believes in internal locus of control.

Believes in anticipating future opportunities and threats.

Believes in recognizing strength and weaknesses.

Believes in establishing priorities to seek best.

Believes in mobilizing vision into accomplishment.

Believes in influencing and inspiring others.

Believes in satisfying self with excellence only.

Believes in abiding with law of equality, common benefit, social justice and confronting discrimination.

Believes in becoming liberal, enterprising, competitive, industrious and committed.

Believes in mutual relationships *i.e.*, symbiosis.

Believes in the principle of "survival of the fittest"

Emerging Leadership Requirements: Transactional to Transformational

More so than previously, business organizations recognize that leadership transcends senior executives, it is the responsibility of organizational system and culture that leader is given autonomy and released from attending to routine tasks in order to have enough time to plan for a new vision and to concentrate their attention on critical issues.

There is a need to explore and find out situations in which leaders are going to be effective and efficient for leading strategic change. The set of skills that make of effectiveness in leadership can be understood with the word VARIANCES, a concept being elaborated in this research on leadership. Developing this frame of mind will enable people to perform leadership roles in more effective manner in all leadership situations. This is due to variances that a leader has as an innate virtue up to an extent as well as acquired to further the true leadership. Leader has to build and nurture a new generation of well-rounded professionals who can work as positive change agents in the new millennium, to attain and sustain corporate leadership.

This theme has been deliberated by and large nowhere in the world (B.L. Bajpai, 2002). It has been in the Trait theory of leadership that leadership involves quality and/or charisma. In essence leadership is a work and not a set of personality traits. The word Variances incorporates,

V Stands for, Vision and Values that is Foresight and one's Predictable Behaviour

A Stands for, Attitude, that is Positive and Proactive.

R Stands for, Relationship that is Mutual Interaction.

I Stands for, Internal Motivation, that is Enthusiasm and Inspiration.

A Stands for, Action Orientation that is Implementation.

N Stands for, no, that is Ability to Boldly Reject.

C Stands for, Courage, Competence, Confidence, Commitment and Continuity.

E Stands for, Emotional Intelligence that is Self-Awareness, Self-Managed, Self-motivated and Empathetic.

S Stands for, Spiritual Intelligence that is Love, Service and Self-Esteem.

How Transformation Takes Place

For implementation of any transformation, the mode of intervention is critical, since no transformation can be a one-shot affair. It is a continuous process encompassing many phases, each phase having its own unique focus.

As organizational culture is the general pattern of behaviour, shared beliefs and values that members have in common. The culture exercises a pervasive influence on the organization's structure, systems, and operating managerial/leadership style. An insight into our cultural milieu and norms will help us evolve styles and management systems, which are best suited to corporate functioning. Over the years it has been observed that Indian organizations are caught in the dilemma of trying to reinvent them without discarding old modes of transacting business. Most of them chant the mantra of transformation however only a few are able to translate the intention into action. The most realistic example of this predilection may be observed in Indian government offices and factories where nothing is discarded.

The basic foundation of architecting in India is power differentiation and therefore Indian organizations are tall and pyramidal. Indian organizations are mostly procedure centric. There is low focus on innovation and excellence. Companies focus more on short term and quick gains rather than creating sustainable competitive advantage. Unfortunately in strategy crafting there is less focus on global perspective and benchmarking. The heavy thrust of strategy formulation is on defending rather than winning. Business organizations in India would be better off if we were to attempt to make the change at the root itself, evolve culturally and functionally to have perfect management system and leadership styles.

In the Indian context, it is certainly important that we search and take a close look at our culture and learn from the available elements of various models, to make some conscious choice about the type of organization we want to build, and the kind of systems we want to develop in the work organization. It will be a great pity if work organizations merely perpetuate the culture they have inherited or the culture, which prevails in society. One should seriously consider how far the argument of conforming to the culture or designing a system to suit the culture takes the organization forward.

Most of the organizations in the private sector are generally one-man show. Often the owner also performs the functions of a manager. This is true not only for the small-scale organization but also for the large ones. Generally the board is constituted to fulfill the legal requirement but real control lies in a single person. Owner-Manager's style of functioning is normally centralized and he believes in more direct control and often discourages professionalisation of management.

In many public sector organizations, the situation is no better. It is an accept fact that managers in many public sector organizations, particularly at higher levels, often greatly borrow the traits of bureaucracy, just as the top level private sector managers carry a family or business house traits, even though they have the facade of professionalisation. Many top-level public sector managers have worked, lived and imbibed the government way of working.

Certain steps are necessary to take a proactive approach, *viz.*, using the existing strengths of the culture, reinforcing them, and establishing new traditions and norms in the organization. It is necessary in the beginning to be quite clear about where the organization wants to go. An open discussion about new directions will help the organization to make the necessary psychological preparation for accepting the system. The system needs changes not only in the orientation and attitudes of the people in the organization, but also in the skills, which, are needed to implement and use the system.

CULTURAL METAMORPHOSIS MODES AND PROCESS

Management of transformation is a culture-specific phenomenon. Corporate transformation will pose question to the top management about the present culture and the type of culture, which should be developed in the future, it is more accurately described as simply an evolution from all that has gone before. To achieve cultural metamorphosis, Indian organizations need to encourage liberal thinking questioning mindsets, quest for experimentation and desire to innovate and constant renewal.

This will enable the organization to become a leader in its own right. The culture generated by that combination of pursuits is charged with energy, commitment, resolve, and zest. An internal dynamism evolves that progressively lifts individual contributions to levels of excellence never before achieved.

The company will demand that employees add value to the organization and align their action in the same direction as the organization heads and employees will demand from the organization, the right to interesting and challenging work, career planning, the freedom and resources to perform it well, suitable training and self-development opportunities, and fair appraisal and rewards. That's why corporate culture could be the most powerful tool that a company has at its disposal for, motivating retaining and getting the best out of its people. For only with a clearly defined culture will CEOs be able to ensure a fit with people who share the same values, morals, priorities and attitudes.

It is with this equation that corporate will have to evolve a culture that motivates and equips its people to deliver quality. So CEOs must ensure that the corporate vision, mission statement, values, and targets are communicated clearly to all employees, equipping them with all the information, means and counseling they need to synchronize their actions with the company, they must extract their feedback using employee satisfaction surveys, and modify organizational systems accordingly. Top management must recognize that it has the responsibility and obligation to provide an environment in which an employee feels free to challenge the system to accomplish goals. Once the employee is committed, the techniques become easy. At the psychological level, working for such an organization increases self-pride, individual commitment and motivation.

Enough attention should be paid to the process of managerial autonomy in the organization, taking steps to make work a source of development and growth for managers rather than being treated merely as an activity for which they are paid. The success of the change strategy, therefore, also depends upon leaders' sensitivity, as well their capacity to respond appropriately. Managers have to be extremely concerned with environmental elements, like stakeholders, government, demographic changes, socio-cultural, economic, political, natural, technological and legal factors, shareholders, employees, customers, industrial groups, competitors, suppliers, trade associations, community, social responsibility and good corporate citizenship to incorporate these in the transacting business, since they contribute to achieving business excellence.

The corporate priority in culture building, therefore will be juxtaposing the company's growth with the individual's growth, evolving in the process, new norms of career planning for its people that involve a partnership between the organization and the individual, so CEOs will have to nurture values that respect participative management. A culture, which promotes maximum level of trust among people working in the organization, openness to discuss issues and deal with problems, mutuality in the sense of establishing relationships according to roles and respect for one another.

If India has to catch up with the rest of the world, we need more and more transformational leadership together with transactional one. There is an argument that applicability of management principles may be limited to a particular situation or culture. The above discussion suggests that management in India is marching fast towards corporate transformation, though a large part of it is still traditional. However, if the time to come, the process of professionalisation of management is likely to be faster because of the increasing complexity of managing business, which is not possible for traditional management, and also because of increasing availability of professionally trained managers.

Limitations of the Study

Scarcity of resources limits the horizon of any study, as researches have to restrict the size of the sample due to practical limitations. Corporate leadership as well as role-efficacy are multidimensional and each dimension of these variables are full unit in it self. Future studies dealing with the single dimensions are desirous. It can be inferred that different organizations require different sets of skills due to the intrinsic structural procedural and environmental difference in their settings. These differences in fact significantly alter the leadership behaviour in various types of organizations. To further validate the findings a large number and varied organizations needed to be included into the sample. Other most obvious limitation of the research is that, the results will depend on how truly subjects respond to the questionnaires.

APPENDIX

ORGANIZATION 1

—	Age Yrs	Education	Exp. Yrs	Gender	Mgmt. Lev	Centra	Integra	Proacti
Age Yrs	1.00							
Education	0.03	1.00						
Exp.Yrs	0.96	0.05	1.00					
Gender	– 0.09	– 0.09	– 0.10	1.00				
Mgmt. Lev	– 0.44	– 0.18	– 0.43	0.17	1.00			
Centra	0.16	– 0.06	0.12	0.31	– 0.15	1.00		
Integra	0.01	– 0.11	0.03	– 0.06	0.22	0.05	1.00	
Proacti	0.07	– 0.09	0.13	0.05	0.12	0.09	0.49	1.00
Creati	0.03	– 0.04	0.11	– 0.11	0.00	0.13	0.40	0.35
Inter Role	0.02	0.00	– 0.01	0.09	0.22	0.08	0.20	0.02
Help.Rel	– 0.10	– 0.03	– 0.11	0.08	0.19	– 0.07	– 0.01	0.17
Superordi	– 0.16	– 0.01	– 0.09	0.01	0.26	0.16	0.43	0.40
Influen	0.06	– 0.04	0.12	0.02	0.11	0.16	0.57	0.72
Grow	0.17	– 0.16	0.22	0.02	0.07	0.16	0.50	0.68
Confron	– 0.14	– 0.10	– 0.08	0.05	0.18	0.05	0.32	0.31
R.E.Tot	0.00	– 0.10	0.06	0.06	0.23	0.26	0.68	0.76
R.E.Ind	0.00	– 0.10	0.06	0.06	0.23	0.26	0.68	0.76
P.Mak	0.23	– 0.11	0.30	– 0.10	– 0.04	0.15	0.08	– 0.05
Vision	0.15	– 0.06	0.23	0.05	– 0.18	0.18	0.14	0.15
Plan	0.00	– 0.08	0.03	– 0.03	– 0.35	0.16	0.14	0.15
Model	– 0.09	– 0.01	– 0.04	0.11	– 0.01	– 0.11	0.13	0.13
Set.Stand	0.07	0.01	0.09	0.09	– 0.27	0.32	– 0.10	0.25

Dev. Sys	0.00	0.13	– 0.04	– 0.02	– 0.09	0.07	0.01	– 0.25
Mon.Per	0.18	– 0.02	0.12	0.00	– 0.03	– 0.11	0.01	– 0.11
B. Mgmt	– 0.18	– 0.24	– 0.18	– 0.04	0.44	– 0.18	0.00	– 0.05
Coordi	0.02	0.20	– 0.02	0.01	– 0.04	– 0.02	– 0.15	– 0.11
Synergi	– 0.02	0.00	0.00	0.02	0.35	– 0.21	– 0.14	0.12
Reward	– 0.12	0.05	– 0.14	– 0.08	0.28	– 0.17	– 0.11	– 0.06
Dev. Tal	– 0.18	0.00	– 0.24	0.04	0.20	– 0.08	– 0.20	– 0.10
Coach	– 0.24	– 0.04	– 0.24	0.00	0.23	– 0.22	– 0.04	0.14
B. Cul Cli	– 0.05	0.02	– 0.08	0.03	0.11	– 0.04	0.00	0.04
Led.Tot	#DIV/0!	#DIV/0!	#DIV/0!	#DIV/0!	#DIV/0!	#DIV/0!	#DIV/0!	#DIV/0!

Creati	*Inter Role*	*Help. Rel*	*Superordi*	*Influen*	*Grow*	*Confron*	*R.E. Tot*	*R.E. Ind*
1.00								
0.22	1.00							
– 0.07	0.10	1.00						
0.16	0.25	0.29	1.00					
0.42	0.13	0.20	0.40	1.00				
0.29	0.12	0.24	0.34	0.60	1.00			
0.05	0.00	0.12	0.32	0.24	0.23	1.00		
0.51	0.37	0.41	0.70	0.78	0.73	0.43	1.00	
0.51	0.37	0.41	0.70	0.78	0.73	0.43	1.00	1.00
0.14	0.08	0.01	0.03	– 0.11	0.25	– 0.07	0.09	0.09
0.06	– 0.04	– 0.09	0.08	0.14	0.14	0.29	0.16	0.16
0.19	0.01	– 0.21	0.18	0.27	0.08	0.21	0.19	0.19
0.15	0.02	– 0.04	0.06	– 0.08	0.01	0.26	0.09	0.09
– 0.13	– 0.29	0.02	0.04	0.19	0.19	0.01	0.08	0.08
– 0.05	0.07	– 0.05	– 0.18	– 0.12	– 0.22	0.23	– 0.12	– 0.12
– 0.13	– 0.12	– 0.02	– 0.28	0.07	– 0.17	– 0.17	– 0.18	– 0.18
0.03	0.01	– 0.07	0.11	– 0.09	– 0.10	– 0.20	– 0.07	– 0.07
– 0.03	– 0.15	– 0.09	– 0.16	0.10	– 0.32	– 0.16	– 0.19	– 0.19
– 0.11	0.00	0.01	0.06	0.09	– 0.06	– 0.10	– 0.03	– 0.03
– 0.07	0.04	0.06	0.11	– 0.22	– 0.02	– 0.08	– 0.06	– 0.06
– 0.19	0.14	0.15	– 0.07	– 0.09	– 0.06	– 0.06	– 0.09	– 0.09
– 0.16	0.02	0.20	0.17	– 0.09	0.09	– 0.15	0.04	0.04
0.07	0.08	0.35	0.06	– 0.09	0.33	– 0.40	0.11	0.11
#DIV/0!	#DIV/0!	#DIV/0!	#DIV/0!	#DIV/0!	#DIV/0!	#DIV/0!	#DIV/0!	#DIV/0!

P. Mak	Vision	Plan	Model	Set. Stand	Dev. Sys	Mon. Per	B. Mgmt	Coordi
1.00								
0.46	1.00							
– 0.14	0.25	1.00						
0.15	0.21	0.07	1.00					
0.03	0.25	0.18	– 0.13	1.00				
– 0.23	– 0.30	– 0.04	– 0.27	– 0.07	1.00			
– 0.26	– 0.34	– 0.13	– 0.35	– 0.06	0.36	1.00		
– 0.13	– 0.28	– 0.21	– 0.15	– 0.33	– 0.41	– 0.06	1.00	
– 0.60	– 0.42	0.03	– 0.32	– 0.15	0.11	0.41	0.23	1.00
– 0.35	– 0.17	– 0.27	– 0.21	– 0.10	– 0.36	0.05	0.53	0.29
0.02	– 0.07	– 0.39	0.25	– 0.26	– 0.48	– 0.54	0.45	– 0.04
– 0.30	– 0.23	– 0.40	– 0.07	– 0.17	0.04	– 0.19	0.05	– 0.13
– 0.04	– 0.15	– 0.39	0.08	– 0.11	– 0.43	– 0.39	0.24	– 0.19
0.33	– 0.17	– 0.34	– 0.19	– 0.07	– 0.22	– 0.11	0.08	– 0.27
#DIV/0!	#DIV/0!	#DIV/0!	#DIV/0!	#DIV/0!	#DIV/0!	#DIV/0!	#DIV/0!	#DIV/0!

	Synergi	Reward	Dev. Tal	Coach	B. Cul Cli	Led. Tot
	1.00					
	0.36	1.00				
	0.18	0.32	1.00			
	0.25	0.53	0.59	1.00		
	– 0.11	0.07	0.07	0.26	1.00	
	#DIV/0!	#DIV/0!	#DIV/0!	#DIV/0!	#DIV/0!	1

ORGANIZATION 2

—	Age Yrs	Education	Exp. Yrs	Gender	Mgmt. Lev	Centra	Integra	Proacti
Age Yrs	1.00							
Education	0.31	1.00						
Exp.Yrs	0.81	0.18	1.00					
Gender	– 0.30	– 0.06	– 0.11	1.00				
Mgmt. Lev	– 0.27	– 0.19	– 0.41	– 0.19	1.00			
Centra	0.02	0.19	0.06	0.06	– 0.04	1.00		
Integra	0.18	– 0.10	0.29	0.18	– 0.05	– 0.18	1.00	
Proacti	0.00	– 0.01	0.04	0.19	– 0.04	0.18	0.31	1.00
Creati	0.17	0.27	0.33	0.13	– 0.23	0.37	0.18	0.37

Inter Role	– 0.07	– 0.05	– 0.01	0.22	0.17	0.41	– 0.13	0.31
Help. Rel	– 0.10	– 0.01	– 0.03	0.18	0.06	0.37	– 0.04	0.46
Superordi	0.13	0.15	– 0.01	– 0.10	– 0.02	0.02	– 0.05	0.13
Influen	– 0.09	0.11	– 0.23	0.01	– 0.22	– 0.04	0.00	0.31
Grow	0.15	0.16	0.16	0.05	– 0.29	0.07	0.11	0.64
Confron	– 0.04	– 0.04	– 0.09	– 0.18	0.13	0.11	0.03	0.12
R.E.Tot	0.09	0.16	0.10	0.14	– 0.11	0.41	0.27	0.76
R.E. Ind	0.09	0.16	0.10	0.14	– 0.11	0.41	0.27	0.76
P.Mak	0.10	0.03	– 0.01	– 0.09	0.24	0.13	– 0.25	0.33
Vision	– 0.04	– 0.15	– 0.15	0.01	0.16	– 0.13	0.09	0.02
Plan	– 0.06	– 0.04	– 0.05	0.08	0.25	– 0.21	0.20	0.07
Model	0.17	– 0.20	0.14	0.11	0.05	– 0.08	0.21	– 0.22
Set. Stand	– 0.09	0.11	– 0.02	0.14	– 0.07	– 0.01	0.23	0.03
Dev. Sys	0.41	0.16	0.32	– 0.22	– 0.06	– 0.13	0.22	– 0.22
Mon.Per	0.07	0.24	0.08	0.03	0.00	0.01	– 0.18	– 0.26
B. Mgmt	0.20	– 0.16	0.02	– 0.09	– 0.07	– 0.29	0.09	– 0.09
Coordi	0.12	0.07	0.16	– 0.18	– 0.07	0.13	0.02	– 0.37
Synergi	– 0.12	– 0.04	– 0.12	– 0.08	– 0.16	0.20	– 0.18	– 0.07
Reward	– 0.06	0.08	– 0.12	0.13	0.08	0.34	– 0.11	0.10
Dev. Tal	– 0.01	0.01	– 0.01	0.00	– 0.26	0.07	– 0.07	– 0.17
Coach	– 0.31	– 0.07	– 0.15	0.32	– 0.12	0.04	– 0.07	0.30
B. Cul Cli	– 0.17	0.03	– 0.02	– 0.12	– 0.11	0.01	– 0.18	0.22
Led. Tot	#DIV/0!	#DIV/0!	#DIV/0!	#DIV/0!	#DIV/0!	#DIV/0!	#DIV/0!	#DIV/0!

Creati	*Inter Role*	*Help. Rel*	*Superordi*	*Influen*	*Grow*	*Confron*	*R.E. Tot*	*R.E. Ind*
1.00								
0.38	1.00							
0.41	0.53	1.00						
0.08	0.05	0.17	1.00					
0.05	– 0.16	– 0.05	0.37	1.00				
0.27	0.19	0.41	0.30	0.19	1.00			
0.00	0.04	0.14	0.11	0.20	– 0.05	1.00		
0.60	0.43	0.61	0.51	0.42	0.62	0.33	1.00	
0.60	0.43	0.61	0.51	0.42	0.62	0.33	1.00	1.00
0.09	0.30	0.44	0.33	0.06	0.16	0.24	0.37	0.37
– 0.11	0.28	0.29	0.24	0.10	– 0.01	0.06	0.16	0.16
– 0.14	0.03	– 0.06	– 0.04	– 0.13	0.11	– 0.03	– 0.03	– 0.03

– 0.36	– 0.19	– 0.31	0.01	– 0.30	– 0.06	– 0.37	– 0.33	– 0.33
0.21	– 0.20	0.08	– 0.04	– 0.02	0.04	0.12	0.08	0.08
– 0.02	– 0.44	– 0.04	0.12	– 0.06	– 0.08	– 0.02	– 0.06	– 0.06
– 0.01	– 0.18	– 0.03	0.14	– 0.04	– 0.22	0.03	– 0.12	– 0.12
– 0.01	– 0.16	– 0.25	– 0.16	0.11	– 0.16	– 0.19	– 0.21	– 0.21
– 0.08	– 0.18	– 0.37	– 0.04	– 0.24	– 0.23	– 0.29	– 0.34	– 0.34
0.11	– 0.03	0.01	– 0.15	0.03	– 0.16	– 0.06	– 0.07	– 0.07
0.12	0.04	– 0.05	– 0.03	0.23	– 0.10	0.02	0.11	0.11
– 0.08	– 0.04	– 0.13	– 0.13	0.04	– 0.09	– 0.02	– 0.14	– 0.14
0.21	0.14	0.11	– 0.42	0.04	0.22	0.03	0.08	0.08
0.07	0.20	0.10	0.10	0.12	0.22	0.22	0.20	0.20
#DIV/0!	#DIV/0!	#DIV/0!	#DIV/0!	#DIV/0!	#DIV/0!	#DIV/0!	#DIV/0!	#DIV/0!

Mak	*Vision*	*Plan*	*Model*	*Set. Stand*	*Dev. Sys*	*Mon. Per*	*B. Mgmt*	*Coordi*
1.00								
0.22	1.00							
0.05	0.16	1.00						
– 0.21	– 0.07	0.39	1.00					
– 0.27	– 0.16	0.20	0.07	1.00				
0.05	0.23	0.21	0.11	0.16	1.00			
0.23	– 0.13	– 0.19	– 0.01	– 0.19	0.10	1.00		
– 0.19	– 0.01	– 0.04	0.10	0.03	0.04	– 0.12	1.00	
– 0.38	– 0.40	– 0.04	0.34	0.03	0.00	– 0.06	– 0.04	1.00
– 0.27	– 0.25	– 0.64	– 0.24	– 0.03	– 0.33	– 0.23	0.12	0.20
– 0.08	– 0.28	– 0.51	– 0.21	0.02	– 0.46	0.13	0.11	0.01
– 0.37	– 0.18	– 0.69	– 0.34	– 0.17	– 0.21	– 0.10	– 0.08	0.06
– 0.15	– 0.18	– 0.06	– 0.29	– 0.03	– 0.30	– 0.31	– 0.14	– 0.23
0.06	– 0.20	– 0.38	– 0.48	– 0.42	– 0.44	0.10	– 0.36	– 0.18
#DIV/0!	#DIV/0!	#DIV/0!	#DIV/0!	#DIV/0!	#DIV/0!	#DIV/0!	#DIV/0!	#DIV/0!

	Synergi	*Reward*	*Dev. Tal*	*Coach*	*B. Cul Cli*	*Led. Tot*
	1.00					
	0.50	1.00				
	0.60	0.30	1.00			
	0.10	– 0.08	0.17	1.00		
	0.04	0.06	0.38	0.28	1.00	
	#DIV/0!	#DIV/0!	#DIV/0!	#DIV/0!	#DIV/0!	1.00

ORGANIZATION 3

—	*Age Yrs*	*Education*	*Exp. Yrs*	*Gender*	*Mgmt. Lev*	*Centra*	*Integra*	*Proacti*
Age Yrs	1.00							
Education	0.46	1.00						
Exp.Yrs	0.95	0.42	1.00					
Gender	0.16	0.05	0.19	1.00				
Mgmt. Lev	– 0.74	– 0.48	– 0.77	– 0.02	1.00			
Centra	0.40	0.16	0.37	– 0.02	– 0.35	1.00		
Integra	0.46	0.21	0.47	0.17	– 0.42	0.22	1.00	
Proacti	0.36	0.30	0.39	0.21	– 0.32	0.37	0.35	1.00
Creati	0.26	0.07	0.20	– 0.01	– 0.23	0.60	0.41	0.47
Inter Role	0.13	0.17	0.16	– 0.26	– 0.15	0.18	0.26	0.25
Help. Rel	0.20	– 0.06	0.25	– 0.06	– 0.31	0.49	0.24	0.26
Superordi	0.47	0.14	0.51	0.15	– 0.38	0.41	0.45	0.49
Influen	0.20	0.04	0.25	– 0.01	– 0.19	0.40	0.00	0.45
Grow	0.16	0.12	0.18	– 0.09	– 0.11	0.41	0.10	0.47
Confron	0.45	0.19	0.46	0.03	– 0.21	0.05	0.31	0.08
R.E.Tot	0.48	0.21	0.50	0.02	– 0.41	0.66	0.49	0.68
R.E. Ind	0.48	0.21	0.50	0.02	– 0.41	0.66	0.49	0.68
P.Mak	– 0.23	– 0.01	– 0.20	– 0.03	0.11	– 0.12	– 0.16	– 0.10
Vision	0.01	0.17	0.03	– 0.08	– 0.17	0.09	0.04	0.08
Plan	– 0.15	0.06	– 0.11	0.15	0.07	– 0.01	– 0.19	– 0.12
Model	0.12	0.11	0.14	0.10	– 0.07	0.06	0.04	0.15
Set. Stand	0.09	0.00	0.06	– 0.10	0.01	0.24	0.12	0.15
Dev. Sys	0.25	– 0.04	0.14	– 0.03	– 0.18	0.01	0.09	– 0.10
Mon. Per	0.14	– 0.03	0.07	– 0.02	– 0.01	– 0.02	0.07	– 0.05
B. Mgmt	– 0.17	0.06	– 0.19	– 0.13	0.17	0.15	– 0.02	0.09
Coordi	0.00	– 0.10	0.00	0.12	0.11	– 0.15	– 0.04	– 0.29
Synergi	0.18	0.08	0.23	0.21	– 0.09	– 0.07	0.09	0.20
Reward	0.13	– 0.13	0.13	– 0.04	– 0.21	0.13	– 0.01	– 0.09
Dev. Tal	0.15	0.05	0.13	0.01	– 0.03	– 0.08	0.22	0.23
Coach	– 0.10	– 0.12	– 0.06	– 0.02	0.15	– 0.25	0.01	0.03
B. Cul Cli	– 0.19	– 0.28	– 0.15	– 0.02	0.11	– 0.12	– 0.13	– 0.19
Led. Tot	#DIV/0!	#DIV/0!	#DIV/0!	#DIV/0!	#DIV/0!	#DIV/0!	#DIV/0!	#DIV/0!

Creati	*Inter Role*	*Help. Rel*	*Superordi*	*Influen*	*Grow*	*Confron*	*R.E. Tot*	*R.E. Ind*
1.00								
0.28	1.00							
0.45	0.42	1.00						
0.58	0.20	0.42	1.00					
0.37	0.36	0.52	0.48	1.00				
0.40	0.35	0.41	0.36	0.60	1.00			
0.18	0.17	– 0.07	0.31	0.10	0.04	1.00		
0.74	0.54	0.66	0.76	0.72	0.68	0.32	1.00	
0.74	0.54	0.66	0.76	0.72	0.68	0.32	1.00	1.00
– 0.36	– 0.15	– 0.17	– 0.08	– 0.12	– 0.06	– 0.25	– 0.23	– 0.23
0.14	– 0.05	0.13	0.15	– 0.05	0.03	0.01	0.09	0.09
– 0.27	– 0.18	– 0.15	– 0.06	– 0.07	0.11	– 0.19	– 0.16	– 0.16
0.07	0.13	0.11	0.04	0.08	0.04	0.04	0.12	0.12
0.30	0.21	0.34	0.22	0.25	0.27	0.07	0.34	0.34
0.23	0.02	0.11	– 0.02	0.09	0.05	0.09	0.08	0.08
0.03	0.18	– 0.13	– 0.04	0.11	0.03	0.10	0.04	0.04
0.08	– 0.01	0.03	– 0.14	– 0.05	– 0.07	0.12	0.01	0.01
– 0.35	– 0.06	– 0.22	– 0.19	– 0.10	– 0.14	– 0.15	– 0.26	– 0.26
0.04	– 0.10	0.12	0.19	– 0.12	– 0.05	– 0.04	0.04	0.04
0.02	– 0.08	0.09	0.05	0.01	– 0.17	0.09	0.00	0.00
0.26	0.10	0.10	0.18	0.18	0.04	0.23	0.23	0.23
– 0.19	0.03	– 0.38	– 0.18	– 0.05	– 0.05	0.04	– 0.16	– 0.16
0.06	0.06	0.05	– 0.08	– 0.10	– 0.17	– 0.06	– 0.11	– 0.11
#DIV/0!	#DIV/0!	#DIV/0!	#DIV/0!	#DIV/0!	#DIV/0!	#DIV/0!	#DIV/0!	#DIV/0!

P.Mak	*Vision*	*Plan*	*Model*	*Set. Stand*	*Dev. Sys*	*Mon. Per*	*B. Mgmt*	*Coordi*
1.00								
0.40	1.00							
0.59	0.27	1.00						
– 0.32	– 0.24	– 0.06	1.00					
– 0.27	– 0.36	– 0.42	0.08	1.00				
– 0.43	– 0.23	– 0.26	– 0.05	0.10	1.00			
– 0.34	– 0.73	– 0.31	0.05	0.35	0.52	1.00		
– 0.42	– 0.22	– 0.27	0.18	0.17	– 0.23	– 0.07	1.00	
– 0.08	– 0.47	– 0.11	– 0.05	– 0.20	0.04	0.31	– 0.12	1.00

– 0.10	0.21	– 0.12	0.22	– 0.18	– 0.29	– 0.56	0.04	– 0.10
– 0.31	– 0.16	– 0.46	– 0.07	0.10	– 0.09	0.04	0.10	0.16
– 0.50	– 0.09	– 0.58	– 0.20	0.21	0.42	0.31	– 0.06	– 0.09
– 0.10	– 0.19	0.05	– 0.22	– 0.39	– 0.13	0.14	0.03	0.24
0.19	0.07	– 0.08	– 0.07	0.07	– 0.02	– 0.20	– 0.16	0.07
#DIV/0!	#DIV/0!	#DIV/0!	#DIV/0!	#DIV/0!	#DIV/0!	#DIV/0!	#DIV/0!	#DIV/0!

	Synergi	*Reward*	*Dev. Tal*	*Coach*	*B. Cul Cli*	*Led. Tot*
	1.00					
	0.09	1.00				
	0.03	0.15	1.00			
	0.00	0.04	0.10	1.00		
	– 0.02	– 0.05	– 0.18	– 0.46	1.00	
	#DIV/0!	#DIV/0!	#DIV/0!	#DIV/0!	#DIV/0!	1.00

ORGANIZATION 4

—	*Age Yrs*	*Education*	*Exp.Yrs*	*Gender*	*Mgmt. Lev*	*Centra*	*Integra*	*Proacti*
Age Yrs	1.00							
Education	– 0.09	1.00						
Exp.Yrs	0.60	– 0.10	1.00					
Gender	0.14	0.05	– 0.32	1.00				
Mgmt. Lev	– 0.38	– 0.47	– 0.57	0.24	1.00			
Centra	0.16	0.19	– 0.10	0.09	– 0.17	1.00		
Integra	– 0.04	0.20	– 0.17	0.12	– 0.16	0.52	1.00	
Proacti	0.12	0.11	0.09	– 0.13	– 0.25	0.45	0.49	1.00
Creati	– 0.13	0.33	– 0.04	– 0.13	– 0.14	0.12	0.50	0.43
Inter Role	0.15	– 0.15	0.27	0.09	– 0.31	– 0.01	0.37	0.10
Help. Rel	0.08	– 0.03	0.16	– 0.29	– 0.26	0.04	0.00	0.18
Superordi	– 0.21	0.14	0.01	– 0.14	– 0.19	– 0.12	0.32	0.02
Influen	– 0.10	– 0.04	– 0.17	– 0.35	– 0.10	0.15	0.25	0.26
Grow	– 0.25	0.22	– 0.27	0.21	0.02	0.15	0.68	0.20
Confron	– 0.20	0.04	– 0.22	0.09	– 0.09	0.05	0.27	– 0.02
R.E. Tot	– 0.09	0.18	– 0.06	– 0.10	– 0.31	0.37	0.77	0.54
R.E. Ind	– 0.09	0.18	– 0.06	– 0.10	– 0.31	0.37	0.77	0.54
P. Mak	0.21	– 0.03	– 0.04	0.14	– 0.11	– 0.01	0.10	0.20
Vision	0.05	– 0.04	0.22	– 0.20	– 0.20	0.14	0.01	0.13

Plan	0.12	– 0.05	– 0.08	0.18	– 0.20	0.10	0.26	0.12
Model	– 0.30	– 0.13	– 0.15	– 0.03	0.17	– 0.16	– 0.10	– 0.17
Set. Stand	– 0.03	– 0.09	0.04	– 0.26	0.11	0.22	– 0.02	0.24
Dev. Sys	– 0.14	– 0.20	– 0.18	0.05	0.27	– 0.16	– 0.04	– 0.29
Mon.Per	0.15	– 0.05	– 0.08	0.26	0.08	0.09	0.19	0.03
B. Mgmt	– 0.13	– 0.09	0.14	– 0.12	0.01	– 0.29	– 0.39	– 0.35
Coordi	– 0.41	0.14	– 0.38	0.14	0.30	– 0.13	0.20	– 0.32
Synergi	0.00	0.22	0.05	– 0.22	0.14	– 0.18	– 0.46	– 0.05
Reward	– 0.11	0.04	0.28	– 0.25	– 0.08	– 0.03	– 0.18	0.08
Dev. Tal	0.09	– 0.03	0.13	– 0.26	0.13	– 0.14	– 0.10	0.03
Coach	0.06	0.24	0.10	0.17	0.00	0.06	– 0.02	0.06
B. Cul Cli	0.13	0.20	0.09	0.02	– 0.25	0.30	0.01	0.00
Led. Tot	#DIV/0!	#DIV/0!	#DIV/0!	#DIV/0!	#DIV/0!	#DIV/0!	#DIV/0!	#DIV/0!

Creati	*Inter Role*	*Help. Rel*	*Superordi*	*Influen*	*Grow*	*Confron*	*R.E. Tot*	*R.E. Ind*
1.00								
0.20	1.00							
– 0.09	0.28	1.00						
0.42	0.27	– 0.05	1.00					
0.35	0.09	– 0.02	0.16	1.00				
0.49	0.19	– 0.10	0.44	0.22	1.00			
0.18	0.33	0.01	0.33	0.58	0.27	1.00		
0.69	0.53	0.22	0.56	0.57	0.62	0.58	1.00	
0.69	0.53	0.22	0.56	0.57	0.62	0.58	1.00	1.00
– 0.06	0.19	– 0.04	– 0.12	0.21	0.05	0.31	0.15	0.15
– 0.05	0.16	0.16	0.12	0.24	– 0.07	0.20	0.19	0.19
0.21	0.37	0.09	0.13	0.28	0.13	0.47	0.41	0.41
0.10	0.12	0.17	0.14	0.14	0.01	0.13	0.09	0.09
– 0.02	– 0.19	0.25	0.11	– 0.08	– 0.15	– 0.09	0.05	0.05
– 0.29	– 0.09	– 0.14	– 0.02	– 0.03	0.03	0.09	– 0.17	– 0.17
0.03	0.05	– 0.03	– 0.06	– 0.12	0.03	– 0.24	– 0.02	– 0.02
– 0.19	0.03	0.09	0.05	– 0.03	– 0.04	– 0.07	– 0.21	– 0.21
0.01	– 0.21	– 0.24	0.10	– 0.18	0.25	0.11	– 0.07	– 0.07
0.03	– 0.57	– 0.15	– 0.13	– 0.14	– 0.29	– 0.59	– 0.45	– 0.45
– 0.06	– 0.25	0.05	– 0.12	– 0.31	– 0.06	– 0.28	– 0.22	– 0.22
0.12	– 0.26	– 0.05	0.17	– 0.04	0.13	– 0.31	– 0.08	– 0.08

0.06	− 0.09	− 0.28	− 0.19	− 0.44	− 0.08	− 0.49	− 0.27	− 0.27
0.07	− 0.01	0.04	− 0.25	− 0.22	− 0.15	− 0.31	− 0.12	− 0.12
#DIV/0!	#DIV/0!	#DIV/0!	#DIV/0!	#DIV/0!	#DIV/0!	#DIV/0!	#DIV/0!	#DIV/0!

P. Mak	*Vision*	*Plan*	*Model*	*Set. Stand*	*Dev. Sys*	*Mon. Per*	*B. Mgmt*	*Coordi*
1.00								
0.09	1.00							
0.70	− 0.06	1.00						
− 0.44	0.04	− 0.30	1.00					
− 0.16	0.21	− 0.17	0.20	1.00				
0.16	− 0.52	0.03	− 0.07	− 0.18	1.00			
− 0.31	− 0.29	− 0.10	− 0.01	− 0.14	− 0.04	1.00		
− 0.57	− 0.18	− 0.48	0.39	− 0.13	0.16	0.06	1.00	
− 0.16	− 0.33	− 0.18	− 0.09	− 0.16	0.41	− 0.01	0.00	1.00
− 0.48	− 0.35	− 0.58	0.10	0.04	0.02	0.11	0.36	− 0.04
− 0.37	0.13	− 0.48	− 0.09	0.03	− 0.04	− 0.33	0.26	− 0.04
− 0.42	− 0.19	− 0.50	0.22	0.13	− 0.04	− 0.07	0.18	0.03
− 0.43	− 0.19	− 0.44	− 0.13	− 0.22	− 0.39	0.31	0.12	0.00
− 0.47	− 0.08	− 0.18	− 0.05	− 0.02	− 0.50	0.12	0.10	− 0.15
#DIV/0!	#DIV/0!	#DIV/0!	#DIV/0!	#DIV/0!	#DIV/0!	#DIV/0!	#DIV/0!	#DIV/0!

Synergi	*Reward*	*Dev. Tal*	*Coach*	*B. Cul Cli*	*Led. Tot*
1.00					
0.27	1.00				
0.50	0.18	1.00			
0.39	0.28	0.21	1.00		
0.16	0.26	0.06	0.62	1.00	
#DIV/0!	#DIV/0!	#DIV/0!	#DIV/0!	#DIV/0!	1.00

ORGANIZATION 5

—	*Age Yrs*	*Education*	*Exp. Yrs*	*Gender*	*Mgmt. Lev*	*Centra*	*Integra*	*Proacti*
Age Yrs	1.00							
Education	0.11	1.00						
Exp. Yrs	0.96	0.14	1.00					
Gender	#DIV/0!	#DIV/0!	#DIV/0!	1.00				

Mgmt. Lev	– 0.25	– 0.49	– 0.32	#DIV/0!	1.00			
Centra	0.32	– 0.01	0.31	#DIV/0!	– 0.20	1.00		
Integra	– 0.10	0.21	– 0.06	#DIV/0!	– 0.28	0.24	1.00	
Proacti	0.13	– 0.05	0.11	#DIV/0!	– 0.33	0.33	0.18	1.00
Creati	0.05	0.01	0.11	#DIV/0!	– 0.21	0.64	0.39	0.32
Inter Role	0.20	– 0.10	0.23	#DIV/0!	– 0.12	0.41	0.27	0.36
Help.Rel	0.14	– 0.13	0.17	#DIV/0!	0.00	0.48	– 0.05	0.18
Superordi	0.02	– 0.12	0.02	#DIV/0!	0.09	0.32	0.26	0.10
Influen	– 0.08	0.20	– 0.10	#DIV/0!	– 0.05	0.30	0.43	0.33
Grow	– 0.21	– 0.24	– 0.23	#DIV/0!	0.13	0.31	0.43	0.21
Confron	0.01	0.29	0.02	#DIV/0!	– 0.14	0.21	– 0.05	0.12
R.E. Tot	0.07	0.01	0.09	#DIV/0!	– 0.18	0.62	0.52	0.45
R.E. Ind	0.06	0.01	0.07	#DIV/0!	– 0.18	0.64	0.52	0.51
P. Mak	– 0.24	– 0.24	– 0.26	#DIV/0!	0.06	0.21	0.19	0.27
Vision	0.04	– 0.04	0.05	#DIV/0!	0.00	0.13	0.34	– 0.01
Plan	– 0.19	– 0.17	– 0.13	#DIV/0!	– 0.03	0.22	0.13	0.19
Model	0.35	0.12	0.35	#DIV/0!	– 0.15	– 0.09	– 0.11	– 0.07
Set. Stand	0.17	0.19	0.18	#DIV/0!	– 0.14	0.17	0.14	0.08
Dev. Sys	– 0.47	– 0.24	– 0.46	#DIV/0!	0.09	– 0.10	0.19	0.27
Mon. Per	0.04	0.20	0.00	#DIV/0!	0.09	– 0.16	0.05	– 0.13
B. Mgmt	0.07	– 0.25	0.00	#DIV/0!	– 0.01	0.16	0.12	0.08
Coordi	0.02	– 0.05	0.02	#DIV/0!	0.02	– 0.09	– 0.26	0.10
Synergi	0.14	– 0.28	0.08	#DIV/0!	0.13	0.12	– 0.06	0.08
Reward	0.07	– 0.25	– 0.04	#DIV/0!	0.08	– 0.07	– 0.27	– 0.25
Dev. Tal	0.02	– 0.02	0.01	#DIV/0!	0.04	– 0.06	– 0.54	– 0.08
Coach	– 0.01	0.10	0.05	#DIV/0!	– 0.23	0.00	– 0.03	0.08
B. Cul Cli	0.10	0.32	0.12	#DIV/0!	0.04	– 0.19	– 0.02	– 0.31
Led.Tot	#DIV/0!	#DIV/0!	#DIV/0!	#DIV/0!	#DIV/0!	#DIV/0!	#DIV/0!	#DIV/0!

Creati	*Inter Role*	*Help.Rel*	*Superordi*	*Influen*	*Grow*	*Confron*	*R.E.Tot*	*R.E.Ind*
1.00								
0.52	1.00							
0.45	0.30	1.00						
0.51	0.39	0.41	1.00					
0.40	0.58	0.13	0.47	1.00				
0.57	0.40	0.36	0.61	0.49	1.00			

0.12	0.22	0.32	0.09	0.38	0.02	1.00		
0.74	0.72	0.55	0.67	0.73	0.70	0.40	1.00	
	0.71	0.54	0.68	0.74	0.72	0.39	0.98	1.00
0.26	0.11	– 0.04	0.08	0.09	0.15	0.06	0.22	0.22
0.35	0.03	0.10	0.43	0.05	0.14	– 0.11	0.21	0.24
0.32	0.27	0.13	0.25	0.34	0.25	0.10	0.34	0.35
– 0.11	0.14	– 0.22	0.15	0.14	– 0.29	0.01	– 0.08	– 0.06
0.20	0.25	0.11	0.41	0.35	0.17	0.12	0.36	0.33
0.06	0.30	– 0.01	0.03	0.28	0.34	0.14	0.23	0.26
– 0.15	– 0.18	0.02	– 0.09	– 0.06	0.04	0.14	– 0.05	– 0.08
0.31	0.21	0.06	0.33	0.09	0.32	– 0.30	0.22	0.22
– 0.10	0.07	0.09	– 0.03	0.11	– 0.02	0.06	0.01	– 0.01
0.01	0.11	– 0.13	– 0.16	– 0.06	0.11	– 0.49	– 0.08	– 0.09
– 0.35	– 0.21	0.06	– 0.29	– 0.25	– 0.09	– 0.12	– 0.31	– 0.31
– 0.33	– 0.33	– 0.06	– 0.31	– 0.34	– 0.47	0.02	– 0.38	– 0.42
– 0.03	0.03	– 0.02	– 0.07	0.00	– 0.33	0.16	– 0.05	– 0.04
– 0.25	– 0.35	– 0.04	– 0.34	– 0.39	– 0.16	– 0.03	– 0.35	– 0.34
#DIV/0!	#DIV/0!	#DIV/0!	#DIV/0!	#DIV/0!	#DIV/0!	#DIV/0!	#DIV/0!	#DIV/0!

P. Mak	*Vision*	*Plan*	*Model*	*Set. Stand*	*Dev. Sys*	*Mon. Per*	*B. Mgmt*	*Coordi*
1.00								
0.42	1.00							
0.23	– 0.06	1.00						
– 0.34	– 0.04	0.11	1.00					
– 0.10	0.25	0.08	0.41	1.00				
0.24	– 0.14	0.23	– 0.02	0.06	1.00			
– 0.18	– 0.18	– 0.36	– 0.44	– 0.38	– 0.14	1.00		
0.12	0.30	– 0.22	– 0.06	0.12	– 0.19	– 0.28	1.00	
– 0.45	– 0.44	0.37	0.22	– 0.14	– 0.14	0.13	– 0.32	1.00
– 0.02	– 0.15	– 0.26	0.05	– 0.04	0.01	– 0.18	0.29	0.00
– 0.04	– 0.16	– 0.29	– 0.17	– 0.22	– 0.22	– 0.10	0.30	– 0.20
– 0.08	– 0.32	– 0.16	0.03	0.07	– 0.17	– 0.31	0.06	– 0.09
0.13	0.01	– 0.24	0.13	– 0.07	– 0.15	– 0.33	0.29	– 0.28
– 0.45	– 0.22	– 0.44	– 0.36	– 0.44	– 0.29	0.67	– 0.32	0.01
#DIV/0!	#DIV/0!	#DIV/0!	#DIV/0!	#DIV/0!	#DIV/0!	#DIV/0!	#DIV/0!	#DIV/0!

Synergi	Reward	Dev. Tal	Coach	B.Cul Cli	Led.Tot
1.00					
0.34	1.00				
0.09	0.22	1.00			
0.00	0.10	0.36	1.00		
− 0.22	0.06	− 0.18	− 0.23	1.00	
#DIV/0!	#DIV/0!	#DIV/0!	#DIV/0!	#DIV/0!	1.00

SENIOR MANAGERS FUNCTIONS SCHEDULE

Name:

Role:

Gender: Date:

Age:

Education:

Experience:

Organization:

Below are given fourteen functions of senior managers. We would like to know how much attention/priority/time you give to these different functions. Each function is defined on a sheet of paper attached with the senior managers function schedule, kindly go through the definition of each function before giving your answers. Distribute your priority/attention/time, assuming it to be 100, among the following functions. The total of all the scores you should give be 100.

Your priority/Attention/time	*Functions*
1.	Policy making
2.	Visioning
3.	Planning
4.	Modelling/Inspiring
5.	Setting standards
6.	Developing systems
7.	Monitoring performance
8.	Boundary management
9.	Coordinating
10.	Synergising
11.	Rewarding
12.	Developing talent/mentoring
13.	Coaching
14.	Building culture and climate
	Total 100

ROLE-EFFICACY SCALE

Name: Role:

Organization: Date:

In each of the following sets of three statements, check the one (*a*, *b* or *c*) that most accurately describes your own experience in your organizational role. You must choose only one statement in each set and put tick mark against it.

1. (*a*) My role is very important in this organization, I feel central here. ______
   (*b*) I am doing useful and fairly important work. ______
   (*c*) Very little importance is given to my role in organization, I feel peripheral here. ______
2. (*a*) My training and expertise are not fully utilized in my present role. ______
   (*b*) My training and knowledge are not used in my present role. ______
   (*c*) I am able to use my knowledge and training very well here. ______
3. (*a*) I have little freedom in my role; I am only an errand boy. ______
   (*b*) I operate according to the directions given to me. ______
   (*c*) I can take initiative and act on my own in my role. ______
4. (*a*) I am doing usual, routine work in my role. ______
   (*b*) In my role I am able to use my creativity and do something new. ______
   (*c*) I have no time for creative work in my role. ______
5. (*a*) No one in the organization responds to my ideas and suggestions. ______
   (*b*) I work in close collaboration with some other colleagues. ______
   (*c*) I am alone and have almost no one to consult in my role. ______
6. (*a*) When I need some help none is available. ______
   (*b*) Whenever I have a problem, others help me. ______
   (*c*) I get very hostile responses when I ask for help. ______
7. (*a*) I regret that I do not have the opportunity to contribute to society in my role. ______
   (*b*) What I am doing in my role is likely to help other organizations or society. ______
   (*c*) I have the opportunity to have some effect on the larger society in my role. ______
8. (*a*) I contribute to some decision. ______
   (*b*) I have no power here. ______
   (*c*) My advice is accepted by my seniors. ______
9. (*a*) Some of what I do contributes to my learning. ______
   (*b*) I am slowly forgetting all that I learned my professional knowledge. ______

(*c*) I have tremendous, opportunities for professional growth in my role. ______

10. (*a*) I dislike being bothered with problems. ______

(*b*) When a subordinate brings a problem to me I help to find a solution. ______

(*c*) I refer the problem to my boss or to some other person. ______

11. (*a*) I feel quite central in the organization. ______

(*b*) I think I am doing fairly important work. ______

(*c*) I feel I am peripheral in this organization. ______

12. (*a*) I do not enjoy my role. ______

(*b*) I enjoy my role very much. ______

(*c*) I enjoy some parts of my role and not others. ______

13. (*a*) I have little freedom in my role. ______

(*b*) I have great deal of freedom in my role. ______

(*c*) I have enough freedom in my role. ______

14. (*a*) I do a good job according to a schedule already decided. ______

(*b*) I am able to be innovative in my role. ______

(*c*) I have no opportunity to be innovative and do something creative. ______

15. (*a*) Others in the organization see my role as significant to their work. ______

(*b*) I am a member of a task force or a committee. ______

(*c*) I do not work in any committees. ______

16. (*a*) Hostility rather than cooperation is evident here. ______

(*b*) I experience enough mutual help here. ______

(*c*) People operate more in isolation here. ______

17. (*a*) I am able to contribute to the company in my role. ______

(*b*) I am able to serve the larger parts of the society in my role. ______

(*c*) I wish I could do some useful work in my role. ______

18. (*a*) I am able to influence relevant decision. ______

(*b*) I am sometimes consulted on important matters. ______

(*c*) I cannot make any independent decision. ______

19. (*a*) I learn a great deal in my role. ______

(*b*) I learn a few new things in my role. ______

(*c*) I am involved in routine or unrelated activities and have learned nothing. ______

20. (*a*) When people bring problems to me, I tend to ask them to work themselves. ______

(*b*) I dislike being bothered with interpersonal conflict. ______

(*c*) I enjoy solving problems related to my work. ______